PRUSSIANISM AND SOCIALISM

PRUSSIANISM

&

SOCIALISM

OSWALD SPENGLER

TRANSLATED AND ANNOTATED BY
CONSTANTIN VON HOFFMEISTER

LEGENDBOOKS

2023

LEGEND
B O O K S

ISBN
PAPERBACK: 978-83-67583-27-5
HARDBACK: 978-83-67583-28-2
EBOOK: 978-83-67583-29-9

www.legendbooks.org

CONTENTS

OSWALD SPENGLER AND THE ARMY BEYOND THE STATE

BY AMORY STERN

LTHOUGH PRIMARILY remembered as a philosopher of history, known to have argued the cyclical theory of civilizations, Oswald Spengler (1880–1936) is secondarily known as one of the premier political theorists of the Weimar German nationalist scene. This milieu produced the philosophical tendency broadly termed the "Conservative Revolution," of which 1919's *Prussianism and Socialism* was Spengler's first published text. By this time, Spengler's debut as a civilizational theorist was well known, but *Prussianism and Socialism* was his first appearance as a political thinker.

1918's first volume of *Der Untergang des Abendlandes* — a project that did not even earn its pessimistic reputation or acquire its English translation title *The Decline of the West* until after the second and final volume was published four years later, in 1922 — had been a vaguely and often indirectly political text. Mostly, in addition to its contribution to the cyclical philosophy of history, the first volume was centered on continuing the long tradition of the Anglo-German feud in the philosophy of science. The latter dispute was an important and oft-overlooked part of modern Western intellectual history, and it stemmed not from when Germany and Britain first became geopolitical rivals, but from the much earlier time of Frederick the Great's comparatively undistinguished grandfather, when Sir Isaac Newton had libeled Gottfried Wilhelm von Leibniz as a plagiarist.[1]

When his successful 1918 debut as a thinker was first published, Spengler was in a mood swinging between optimism spurred by the successful conquest of Russia's Empire in Europe by the Ludendorff-Hindenburg para-regency (a better term for the generals' 1916–1918 control of the *Kaiserreich* than the frequently but questionably applied "dictatorship") on the one hand, and despairing uncertainty about Germany's success on the Western Front on the other. It was amidst the chaos of post-WWI Germany that Spengler adopted his pessimistic intellectual and literary persona and his polemical political theories as a luminary of Germany's Conservative Revolutionary milieu. *Prussianism and Socialism* marks Spengler's debut in both categories, and thus serves as an important intellectual-historical bridge between the first and second volumes of *The Decline of the West.*

During the First World War, when the first volume of his early magnum opus was written, Spengler's political views were more bourgeois-based and open to democratization than they would become following Germany's defeat. The first volume of *The Decline of the West,* published in the summer of 1918, focuses more on aesthetic criticism and the philosophy of science than political polemics. Intellectual biographer John Farrenkopf has shown that Spengler was not always the arch-critic of democracy he became after the war. Rather, notes

---

1   This subject is discussed in Luke Hodgkin, *A History of Mathematics: From Mesopotamia to Modernity* (Oxford University Press, 2005). See Hodgkin quoted in Amory Stern, "Faust Without Mephistopheles: Oswald Spengler and the German Philosophy of Science," in *Conservative Revolution: Responses to Liberalism and Modernity, Volume Two,* ed. Troy Southgate (Black Front Press, 2022), pp. 35–36.

Farrenkopf, during the war, Spengler was an "opportunistic advocate of the quasi-democratization of the Second Reich."[2]

It is not that Spengler ever actually subscribed to the kind of liberal ideals he would later actively scorn, but, during the First World War, he believed that both democratization and imperialism were to be embraced as the unstoppable results of cyclical cultural decline. His known hostility to parliamentarianism had not yet formed during this time. The events that shaped the political views that Spengler is remembered for would begin in late 1918, after the first volume of *The Decline of the West* had recently been published.

The broadly leftist revolution that would sweep Germany started in October of 1918, with a mutiny by German sailors. By November, when Germany sought an armistice, the revolution spread throughout many sectors of the country, including some soldiers. That month, the vanquished Kaiser Wilhelm II was forced to abdicate the throne, and a republic was declared in Germany.

Explains one historian, this revolution would subsequently be divided between the new Social Democratic heads of the government, for whom "the Kaiser's abdication marked the successful end of the revolution," and the more extreme groups for which "the revolution was only the first step."[3] The following year would be marked by much internecine violence in Germany, and only the Social Democrats' uneasy alliance with the nationalist paramilitary movement known as the Freikorps (Free Corps) prevented the country from falling to a Communist takeover. Underneath the surface, notes this source, "many Free Corps members hated both the fledgling Republic and the Socialist Party little less than they did the Communists."[4]

---

2   John Farrenkopf, *Prophet of Decline: Spengler on World History and Politics* (Baton Rouge: LSU Press, 2001), p. 113.

3   Carlos Caballero Jurado, *The German Freikorps, 1918–23* (Botley, Oxford: Osprey Publishing Ltd., 2001), p. 6.

4   Ibid, p. 9.

1919 also saw Germany forced to sign the humiliating and desta-
bilizing Treaty of Versailles. Farrenkopf describes how the aftermath
of World War I changed Spengler's political views. From his earlier
quasi-democratic sensibilities, Germany's fate transformed Spengler
into a thinker for whom "only the overthrow of the Weimar Republic,
a regime illegitimate in its inception in his eyes, and its replacement
with a more authoritarian one, would put Germany back on the path
of power politics and imperialism in the grand style."[5] It was a widespread attitude that would also result in daring lives of political crime,
such as that of General Erich Ludendorff's early Weimar career, or
even the dangerous Freikorps-affiliated assassin gang known as the
"Organisation Consul."

In the fateful year of 1919, Spengler wrote a political polemic called
Prussianism and Socialism. This tract marked his transition to the
political philosophy that would be fully articulated by the time the
second volume of *The Decline of the West* appeared in 1922. It was during these tumultuous years that he became a staunch critic of liberal
democratic ideas, which he rejected both as delusional and as alien to
Germany. At the same time, Spengler recognized that the pre-WWI
Prussian respect for the state and its laws was impossible to recover.

Spengler located the cradle of the political values he despised in
England, which he considered, with backhanded admiration, to be the
only country in which liberal sensibilities ever amounted to a serious
political tradition. (In this regard, Spengler viewed the United States as
an offshoot of the English tradition.) Additionally, Spengler deplored
the influence of Marxism on German political life, which had culminated in the leftist revolutionary activity of 1918 and 1919. *Prussianism
and Socialism* presents the Prussian tradition, under which Germany
had been unified, as pointing to an alternative to both the liberal and
the Marxist orientations.

---

5   Farrenkopf, *Prophet of Decline*, p. 132.

Spengler connects the two philosophical opponents by emphasizing the influence of Karl Marx's (effectively, if not officially) adopted England on Marxist thinking. The text exhibits the contempt for ideologues that would mark all of Spengler's later political writings. To Spengler, "socialism" does not describe an ideology, but an archetype. Spengler depicts this "socialistic" archetype as latent in the historical tradition that *Prussianism and Socialism* hearkens back to.

Spengler's idea of the Prussian tradition as the opposite of a plutocratic archetype builds upon economic philosophies that had been developed in the generations before Spengler's 1918 intellectual debut. It was the now-overlooked philosopher and economist Eugen Dühring who had pioneered the Prussian socialist doctrine as a sociopolitical idea in the 19th century. It was Werner Sombart in 1915 who had given it a militaristic and Nietzschean style. But it was Spengler in 1919's *Prussianism and Socialism*, after the Prussian monarchy had been officially shattered, who first liberated the Prussian ideal from any reference to a concrete state, focusing on it purely as an archetype instead. This changed the definition of "Prussian socialism" to mean something above and beyond the modern state, and that is a significant difference from Spengler's predecessors.

Professor Dühring is known mostly for his negatively received but profound influences on both Friedrich Engels and Friedrich Nietzsche, but Dühring is a forgotten giant in his own right. "Like the anti-democratic thinkers of the Weimar Republic, both Conservative and Socialist," notes Dühring's intellectual biographer and translator Alexander Jacob, "Dühring considered parliamentarism as an outmoded and dangerous system."[6] Dr. Jacob describes Dühring's political thought thus:

> The coalitions of communes formed by workers will guarantee the access of all to property and means of production. The focus is shifted away from the

---

6   Eugen Dühring, *Eugen Dühring on the Jews*, trans. Alexander Jacob (Nineteen Eighty Four Press, 1997), from Jacob's introduction, p. 11.

concept of personal property altogether to relations of the right of use of property according to personal capacity. The precondition for the success of such workers' coalitions, however, is the direction of all their efforts to the interests of the whole, of the public as a totality, and this can be effected perfectly only when the state enters in their support... The leadership of the state can be accomplished only by the prevalence of another sense than that of profit-making such as is directive in the British political economy and in that of its followers on the continent.[7]

Dühring's idea of a revolutionary change in property relations was not synonymous with the Communist ideal of outright abolition of private property. Although Dühring was more sympathetic to the working class than the bourgeoisie, he rejected any kind of class egoism altogether. Thus, he came to reject Marxism as strongly as he did the capitalist status quo. Dühring used the term "Socialitarianism" to describe his own brand of socialism, as distinct from the Marxist variety.[8]

Dühring differed from his Weimar German Conservative Revolutionary successors, such as Spengler, in that Dühring did not share "their identification with the upper classes and their sympathy with the original, if not the present, Prussian elite. Unlike Dühring, too, they were not pacifists and encouraged militarism as a significant political ideal."[9] However, this dislike of war did not prevent Dühring from admiring Frederick the Great and the Prussian tradition as important inspirations for what he considered a "Socialitarian" political economy.

Dühring is an important precursor to Spengler in another way. Dühring, like Schopenhauer before him, attempted to discredit the liberal notions of "progress" at a more scientific than mystical level. Like Goethe, whom he has sometimes been wrongly described as thoroughly disliking, Dühring advocated a finitist view of mathematics

---

7   Ibid, from Jacob's introduction, p. 12.

8   Ibid, from Jacob's introduction, p. 16.

9   Ibid, from Jacob's introduction, p. 34.

and other physical sciences. In this way, Dühring prefigured Spengler's philosophy of science.

As early as the first volume of *The Decline of the West*, that book's readers will recall, Spengler ascribes the finite scientific ethos of Goethe and Dühring (also notably shared by George Berkeley and Edgar Allan Poe) to the ancient Greco-Roman culture and civilization. As bellicosely as Spengler's debut glorifies the modern infinitesimal systems of the Gothic-modern "Faustian" West as historically superior to the physical sciences of what he terms the ancient Greco-Roman "Apollonian" culture, the book is poetically but evocatively ambivalent as to which of these scientific styles is actually closer to the truth. (Dühring's underlying sociopolitical reason for arguing this scientific and metaphysical position also prefigures early National Socialist economic theorist Gottfried Feder's 1919 argument contrasting the profits of the Rothschild and Krupp enterprises: "loan-interest capital... rises far above human conception and strives for infinity... The curve of industrial capital on the other hand remains within the finite!"[10])

The Nietzschean influences on Spengler's theories of time also point to Dühring's intellectual innovations. According to Rudolf Steiner, Nietzsche's philosophy of time, as known through his idea of the eternal recurrence, was heavily influenced by Dühring's philosophy of science. Steiner's argument is lent credibility by the work of Dühring's student in Berlin, Romanian poet and editorialist Mihai Eminescu.

Eminescu had never heard of the then-obscure Nietzsche, but shared Dühring's love of Schopenhauer. Steiner's claim is strengthened by a reading of Eminescu's 1883 poem "Gloss" or "Glossa," in which Dühring's Romanian pupil expresses the *Ur*-Nietzschean view of time at least as eloquently as Nietzsche himself did. "All is old and all is

---

10 Gottfried Feder, *Manifesto for Breaking the Financial Slavery to Interest*, trans. Alexander Jacob (London: Black House Publishing, 2016), p. 38.

new," reads Eminescu's refrain in more than one English translation, surely reflecting the pioneering poet's education under Dühring.[11]

That a German tradition of neo-Heraclitean thought can be identified from Eminescu's German influences to Spengler is observable in another line by Eminescu. "We see what ceased to be!" reads this line in one English version of a short 1886 poem, the title of which has been translated as "To the Star" and — rendered into the language of Eminescu's favorite modern Western culture by Christian W. Schenk — as "*Zum Stern*."[12] Additionally, Eminescu's editorials often articulate what Professor Dühring called his "Socialitarian" ideas on political economy. "Labor is the basis of political economy," argues an article by Dühring's most distinguished Eastern European student, who adds that "any professional institution can only rely on the reality

---

11   Mihai Eminescu, *The Legend of the Evening Star & Selected Poems & Prose*, trans. Adrian George Sahlean (Global Arts Inc., 2020, 2021), pp. 17–21.

   The otherwise quite different 1970s version "Gloss," by the short-lived teen-aged prodigy Corneliu Popescu, also translates Eminescu's phrase as "All is old and all is new." This translation can easily be found online. Popescu's interpretation of Eminescu's epic poem "Luceafarul," controversially titled "Lucifer," is radically different from Sahlean's translation "The Legend of the Evening Star," but both versions depict a vision of the Titan as a misunderstood celestial and solaresque archetype.

12   Ibid, p. 25. For German translations of Eminescu's poetry, see Mihail Eminescu, *Die schönsten Gedichte*, trans. Christian W. Schenk (Dionysos, 2019).

   Of note is that Eminescu admired not only Schopenhauer but also Richard Wagner and especially Friedrich Hölderlin. (Martin Heidegger would later name Hölderlin as Nietzsche's only precursor in seeing past the modern humanist interpretations of the ancient Greeks.) Like Spengler in the following century, Eminescu's work often deals with the Heraclitean orientation of the primacy of eternal becoming. However, in place of Spengler's Goethean and Nietzschean clichés of this pre-Socratic philosophical orientation as amounting to an organic archetype, Eminescu's poetry represents it as a solar or astral one — as Heraclitus himself probably had, especially to the extent that the controversial fire-air-water-earth cycle attributed to Heraclitus is authentic. See Eminescu's "To the Star" (Popescu and Sahlean) or "*Zum Stern*" (Schenk), originally written in Romanian in 1886 as "*La steaua*."

of labor."[13] In the following century, starting with *Prussianism and Socialism* and continuing to his last written works, Spengler would affirm both the fiery Heraclitean idea of life and skepticism toward capitalistic ethics as proud German callings.

Another influence on Spengler's political thought, acknowledged at times even by the notoriously citation-shy Spengler, was the Wilhelmine German economist and sociologist Werner Sombart. "Although Sombart began his sociological career as a socialist in the Marxist vein," explains translator Alexander Jacob, "he gradually dissociated himself from the economic orientation of Marx's social theory in favour of a more voluntarist understanding of the springs of social evolution which supported the traditional and aristocratic model of society that Marx had sought to destroy."[14] Earlier than Spengler, Sombart lauded German militarism as an anti-plutocratic tradition, in contrast to the liberal capitalism associated with England.

This difference would be the theme of Sombart's 1915 wartime manifesto *Traders and Heroes: Patriotic Reflections.* At least as far back as early modern times, argues Sombart, the English mentality has been notable for a "marked tendency to physical comfort, to material well-being," a "pronounced acquisitiveness," "usurious businesses," and "obscurantism."[15] Furthermore, Sombart argues that "all scientific thought in England, if it is not born of a commercial spirit, is still borne by and infused with it." In Sombart's estimation, "the English biology and evolutionary doctrine that has become so famous is basically nothing else but the transference of liberal-bourgeois views to

---

13   Mihai Eminescu, *Old Icons, New Icons*, trans. Tatiana Danilova and Alexandra Meyer (Amory Stern; San Diego, 2020) pp. 104 & 108, cited in Amory Stern, "Mihai Eminescu: Precursor to the Conservative Revolution," in *Conservative Revolution: Responses to Liberalism and Modernity, Volume Two*, ed. Troy Southgate (Black Front Press, 2022), p. 114.

14   Werner Sombart, *Traders and Heroes: Patriotic Reflections,* trans. Alexander Jacob (Arktos Media Ltd., 2021), from Jacob's foreword.

15   Sombart, *Traders and Heroes*, Ch. 1.

the life-processes of nature."[16] Compare the latter quote to what has been noted above about Spengler's philosophy of science, starting from the beginning of his career.[17]

Whereas Dühring had preceded and influenced Nietzsche, Sombart added a Nietzschean influence to the nascent doctrine of Prussian socialism. Like Spengler after him, Sombart absorbed Nietzsche's influence as it was seen in Germany in the first half of the 20th century, which was quite a bit different from the defanged and de-Germanized interpretation of Nietzsche known to post-WWII academic discourse. Today's universities and bookstores tend to treat Nietzsche as a standalone thinker, while the pre-WWII German reception of Nietzsche's thought viewed him as a product of his century and his country. (The latter approach makes more sense, not least because Nietzsche's own philosophy does not allow so easily for such a thing as a cultureless or ahistorical standalone thinker.)

In *Traders and Heroes*, Sombart affirms Nietzsche's Germanness. To Sombart, Nietzsche continued a long tradition of German thinkers. In Sombart's view, "Nietzsche was only the last who spoke to our conscience, perhaps with different words, but in the same sense as all our great Germans before him and as, indeed, only a German could ever speak, even when he wished to be considered rather as a 'good European.'"[18] Although *Traders and Heroes* was written long before the notion of Nietzsche as an idiosyncratic thinker even became commonplace, Sombart already stridently warns against such a reading of Nietzsche. Spengler would later similarly place Nietzsche in a grand tradition of German thinking.

According to Sombart, England and Germany represent mutually antagonistic ideas of civilization. "Trader and hero: they form the two

---

16   Ibid, Ch. 2.

17   See also Amory Stern, "Faust Without Mephistopheles: Oswald Spengler and the German Philosophy of Science," in *Conservative Revolution: Responses to Liberalism and Modernity, Volume Two*, pp. 46–47.

18   Sombart, *Traders and Heroes*, Ch. 5.

great opposites, form as it were the two poles of all human orientation on earth."[19] To Sombart, his definition of heroism is best embodied in this quote from the great German poet Friedrich Schiller: "Life is not the highest of possessions."[20] This life-contemptuous and sacrificial ethos, in Sombart's view, is incomprehensible to a society based on the capitalistic "trader" outlook.

"No heroism without a fatherland," declares Sombart in *Traders and Heroes*, "but as one must equally say: no fatherland without heroism." To Sombart, this idea of the fatherland "has nothing to do with the national pride of the English that is without any spiritual and moral foundation."[21] Sombart affirms German militarism as the opposite of what he considers the shallow commercialism of England: "Militarism is the manifestation of German heroism. Militarism is the realisation of heroic principles... Militarism is the heroic spirit heightened to the warrior spirit."[22] Sombart's concept of a fundamental opposition between militarism and plutocracy would reappear, more refined, in Spengler's *Prussianism and Socialism* four years later.

In *Prussianism and Socialism*, Spengler writes of "the State" as chiefly the calling of the Prusso-German tradition, and the liberal English tradition as its greatest enemy. Yet Spengler's reverence for the tradition of the state strikes a mournful rather than triumphal tone. In Spenglerian terms, he is describing the historical state as already a "thing-become," particularly in light of the Prussian monarchy's recent downfall.

The archetypal ideal of the state he calls upon to regenerate Germany cannot, in Spengler's philosophy of time, return to the same form it had taken before its defeat. This irreversibility would be revealed more explicitly in the second volume of *The Decline of the West*.

---

19 Ibid, Ch. 5.

20 Ibid, Introduction.

21 Ibid, Ch. 6.

22 Ibid, Ch. 8.

Spengler's idea of the recent death of the modern state, without the death of the Prussian ideal as an archetype, must be viewed as bound to the circumstances of contemporary Germany.

The Freikorps fighters, remember, got their start officially enforcing the law of a new republic they never believed in. To them, the Weimar Republic was a treasonous puppet of the victorious Entente powers, with their new liberal order of international law. This sentiment would be exacerbated by the Freikorps troops' experience on the Baltic front of the Russian Civil War in 1919. It was there that they first ventured into their legendary illegality, and their war against the threat of Communist revolution would become a revolution in its own right.

In 1919, the Freikorps intervened in the newly independent Baltic states, expelling the advancing Red Army from Riga, Latvia. In this region of Europe, the ethnic German minorities of the Baltic countries had formed the ruling classes since the Teutonic colonization of the Middle Ages. The Russian Empire had protected their privileges ever since Peter the Great annexed the Baltic region in the early 18th century, but their safety was threatened by the Bolshevik Revolution and the Russian Civil War. The Bolsheviks had overrun the Baltic countries, and most Latvians supported the former out of a vengeful attitude toward the German aristocracy.

Freikorps veteran Ernst von Salomon, in his novelized memoir *The Outlaws*, describes the Bolshevik persecution from which he and other Freikorps fighters intervened to protect the Baltic Germans:

> There was not a single family from which at least one member had not been carried off or tortured or killed. Often whole families had been exterminated together with their servants; in other cases none but a few of the women were left alive and these only the older ones. Things had come to such a pass that anyone who spoke German out in the streets was liable to be slaughtered out of hand; the word "German" was regarded as

an abominable insult, and the Germans themselves as the most loathsome spawn of the earth.[23]

After beating the Bolsheviks out of Riga in 1919, the Freikorps forces planned to turn the Baltic region into a German nationalist base of operations, explains one source, "from where they would reconquer a defeated and humiliated Germany."[24] They also aimed to use this prospective Baltic stronghold "to crush the Soviets, establishing a pro-German government in Russia."[25] This contradicted the orders of Germany's provisional government, which had only aimed to stop the Bolshevik advance toward East Prussia.

Accordingly, many Freikorps fighters illegally volunteered under the White Russian officer Col. Prince Pavel Bermondt-Avalov, who had not forgotten that "throughout centuries of Russian rule in the region the German-Balts had been loyal subjects of the Tsar."[26] Although this Russo-German force failed to conquer Riga from newly independent Latvia due to British intervention, it represented the first serious defiance by the Freikorps of the Weimar government. It would not be the last.

Having tasted the freedom of illegality, many Freikorps veterans of 1919's Baltic theater of the Russian Civil War would help temporarily overthrow the Weimar Republic in early 1920. Since the summer of 1919, a plot had formed under the direction of none other than General Erich Ludendorff, who shared the Freikorps' view of the Weimar state as an illegitimate and treasonous entity. One Ludendorff biographer notes that although the WWI general "remained in the background of the plot," he oversaw and helped fund it, and was accurately described by a Weimar government official as the "theater director" of the

---

23 Ernst von Salomon, *The Outlaws*, trans. Ian F. D. Morrow (United Kingdom: Arktos Ltd., 2013), Ch. 6 ("Advance"), pp. 60–61.

24 Jurado, *The German Freikorps 1918–23*, p. 20.

25 Ibid, p. 19.

26 Ibid, p. 21.

ensuing coup.[27] Another historian finds that Ludendorff was accused, with reason, of being "the father of the Kapp Putsch" by the Weimar Republic's secret police.[28] It was in the outcome of Ludendorff's plot that the Freikorps first actively attacked the Weimar government.

In March of 1920, the Freikorps stormed Berlin and forced the Weimar government into brief exile, installing the nationalist civil servant Wolfgang Kapp as Chancellor. However, the Weimar government exploited the putschists' unpopularity with Germany's workers and their movements by calling for a general strike. This meant the insurrectionists faced deadly opposition from a de facto alliance between the Weimar state and various Communist organizations and other ultra-leftist groups.

Salomon recalls in *The Outlaws* that during their participation in the Kapp Putsch, a Freikorps comrade remarked to him that "the workers are fools. We were fools too when we were fighting for law and order. Now they are fools."[29] Although the Kapp Putsch failed to establish a nationalist state in Germany, and the Weimar government's authority was quickly restored, the bloody experience instilled in Salomon and other Freikorps fighters an even more revolutionary temperament.

After the failure of the Kapp Putsch, a shadowy assassin gang developed from a former Freikorps unit. Salomon's *The Outlaws* depicts his leading role in the underground group, though a memoir of such illegal activities obviously cannot be expected to tell us everything the author knows. One historian of this period has been summarized as characterizing the Organisation Consul, or O.C., as "a murder organization which dispensed sudden death to 'traitors'

27 Jay Lockenour, *Dragonslayer: The Legend of Erich Ludendorff in the Weimar Republic and Third Reich* (Cornell University Press, 2021), p. 87.

28 Michael Kellogg, *The Russian Roots of Nazism: White Émigrés and the Making of National Socialism, 1917–1945* (Cambridge: Cambridge University Press, 2005), p. 102.

29 Salomon, *The Outlaws*, Ch. XII ("Putsch"), p. 152.

by means of *Femgerichte* or vigilante courts supposedly modeled upon medieval progenitors."[30] The Organisation Consul assassinated various Marxists, liberals, and French-backed Bavarian secessionists throughout Germany in the early 1920s.

The Organisation Consul was behind the 1922 assassination of Weimar German Foreign Minister Walther Rathenau. Although considered a liberal nationalist of sorts, the wealthy and respected industrialist Rathenau was targeted by the O.C. for his comparatively acquiescent policy toward the victorious Versailles powers. One scholar explains that within the broader O.C. group, the perpetrators of high-profile assassinations like that of Rathenau "belonged to a small group of conspirators; the bulk of the membership took no part in the murders and had no foreknowledge of them."[31] For his role in the killing, Salomon served five harsh years in prison, also recalled in *The Outlaws,* before being released on a political clemency.

The Freikorps and the Organisation Consul shared with Ludendorff as well as Spengler the vision that what ought to replace the modern state is a new political form, aimed at transforming the famous contemporary description of Frederick the Great's Prussia — that of an "army with a country" — into a concrete reality, and not just a quip. This Weimar German nationalist trend ultimately fizzled politically, and would be outmaneuvered by Hitler's more traditionally statist movement by the 1930s. It is noteworthy that National Socialism had itself sprung from a group that embodied the Weimar nationalist mystique of an army with a country, but this sheer paramilitarism later largely gave way to demagogic methods after the NSDAP became a Hitler cult of personality.

The early NSDAP of Lieutenant Max von Scheubner-Richter and General Ludendorff had essentially been an insurgent paramilitary with a political party, but after Hitler's 1924 prison time for the Beer

---

30   Howard Stern, "The Organisation Consul," *The Journal of Modern History,* 35, no 1 (March 1963), p. 20.

31   Ibid, p. 20.

Hall Putsch, the organization moved closer to favoring a takeover from within the Weimar system. Notably, Hitler triumphed over Ludendorff as the party's master by 1925 because the distinguished general lacked the Austrian's popular charisma. The latter quality, an essentially democratic (or at least, democratized) one, had not mattered as much to the kind of organization the NSDAP had originally developed as. Thus, National Socialism initially sprang from the paramilitaristic tendency identified here as Weimar-era German nationalism, but deviated from it after the Beer Hall Putsch of 1923.

The Weimar generation of German nationalists was unique in its vision of an army beyond the state. This contrasted not only with the established understanding of the term "conservatism," but also in significant ways with the traditionally statist orientation of Fascism, as the latter was understood through its seminal Italian example. In this, Weimar German nationalism had few parallels in interwar Europe, but some draw comparisons.

In Spain, José Antonio Primo de Rivera's Falange aimed to rule the country not primarily by the modern tradition of statist methods, but by Primo de Rivera's idea of an anti-capitalist corporation. "The deification of the State is the exact opposite of what we desire," declared Primo de Rivera.[32] Spain, it is worth noting, is where *Prussianism and Socialism* places the cradle of the first historic "Faustian" Western attempt at building a global empire — and the corresponding first development of a worldview up to such a task. Primo de Rivera was familiar with Spengler's work, and cited it.

In another part of Europe, included in Spengler's model with Russia as a nascent future civilization rather than a part of the "Faustian" Western one, Corneliu Zelea Codreanu and his Legionary movement (alternately known as the Iron Guard) of Romania similarly disdained the modern bureaucratic state. Codreanu aimed for his movement to rule Romania not through the machinery of the

---

32   Nick W. Sinan Gregor, ed., *Jose Antonio Primo de Rivera: The Foundations of the Spanish Phalanx* (KDP Publishers, 2018), p. 73.

state, but by serving as a sort of anti-corruption mafia, as it were. It was thus that Codreanu could insist that he rejected both democracy and dictatorship. Spengler's work would be cited as a major influence by some of Codreanu's followers, such as the fallen nationalist Spanish Civil War volunteer Vasile Marin, and the future 20th-century intellectual giants E. M. Cioran and Mircea Eliade.

By the time of the Second World War, this interwar-era vision of nationalism beyond the state had not made it to power anywhere in Europe. The Falange and the Iron Guard had fallen into ruin after the untimely deaths of their charismatic founders in the 1930s. The Weimar German nationalist dream of an army beyond the state, as noted above, had given way to Hitler's statist tactics. World War II was a war between what ultimately amounted to political forms recognizable as modern states, if in some ways unusual ones. Yet the Weimar generation's notions of post-state armies have proven prescient.

The idea of the army beyond the state was born not only from Germany's internal strife in the aftermath of WWI, but also from the related and little-remembered German role in the Russian Civil War. The outcome of 1920's above-summarized Kapp Putsch caused Lenin to abandon his Central European Communist allies. Lenin had initially hoped to see Bolshevism prevail in Hungary and Germany. "Ever since its foundation," notes one historian, the Communist Party of Germany "had closely followed the orders received from Moscow through the Comintern (the Communist International)."[33]

But in 1919, the Romanians toppled the short-lived Communist dictatorship of Béla Kun in Hungary, while the Freikorps heavily damaged the Communist Party of Germany (KPD) and drove the Red Army out of the Baltic states. The Freikorps, Romania, and Poland halted the Bolshevik advance into Central Europe independently of each other throughout 1919. According to one pro-Bolshevik historian, it was the events of the Kapp Putsch the following year — which failed

---

33 Jurado, *The German Freikorps 1918–23*, p. 28.

to establish a right-wing German government, but also culminated in embarrassing blunders by the KDP — that led a formerly supportive Lenin to denounce Kun and the KPD as tactically foolish and "too far to the left."[34]

It was in this context that Lenin wrote a 1920 book entitled *"Left-Wing" Communism: An Infantile Disorder.* The book's publication marked the split between Leninist Russia and the "left Communism" found in European countries. The results of the Kapp Putsch thus decisively closed the series of fronts of the Russian Civil War that had spilled over westward, far beyond Russia itself. Bolshevism had lost the war for Central Europe.

With Lenin's Bolshevist Russia no longer an immediate threat to Germany, the Freikorps increasingly focused on the then-significant German diaspora within the borders of Poland — by that time an independent country supported by the victorious Entente powers. Even the part of the Silesia region that the disarmed Germany had been granted by the Treaty of Versailles was contested by the emboldened Poles. It occurred to many German nationalists, including Spengler, that their anti-Bolshevism should be balanced with the Prussian orientation toward Russia, a tradition hearkening back to the mature Frederick the Great. This interest would later be expanded upon in Spengler's 1922 lecture "Russia's Double Face."

In "Russia's Double Face," Spengler — notwithstanding his earlier assessment in *Prussianism and Socialism* of what he considered the more political than military causes of Germany's WWI defeat — criticizes the foreign policy blunder of Wilhelmine Germany in making an enemy of Russia. Even Spengler's view of Otto von Bismarck's increasing distance from Russia after the 1878 Congress of Berlin seems ambivalent. "Russia's Double Face" nevertheless invokes Bismarck's subsequently unheeded insistence on avoiding war with Russia.

---

34 Rob Sewell, *Germany: From Revolution to Counter-Revolution* (London: Wellred Books, 1988), Ch. 4.

Even in the first volume of *The Decline of the West,* published in the optimistic 1918 mood spurred by Germany's short-lived Brest-Litovsk empire, Spengler had depicted the Russians and broadly related peoples as akin to the Romanized Germanics of future centuries — that is, bearers of a new high culture. A similar view, by the way, was probably shared by the key conqueror of the vast Brest-Litovsk space — and a major father of modern Belarus — General Ludendorff himself.[35] This parallel with Ludendorff is significant to a proper understanding of Spengler's respectful attitude toward the Russians, insofar as Spengler was always an ardent exponent of the Heraclitean idea that war is the father of all, from his doctoral thesis on Heraclitus to his posthumously published mature theories of anthropology.

Ludendorff had learned the Russian language before WWI. Though he had still dismissed anti-Semitism as irrational in 1916, Ludendorff likely picked up his anti-Semitism and his interest in conspiratorial subjects from his Russian Civil War partnership with the outspokenly Germanophile White Russian segment circled around Vladimir M. Purishkevich.[36] (In the 1900s, Purishkevich had been a close associate of fellow Russified Moldavian Pavel Krushevan, recently identified by historian Steven J. Zipperstein as the first editor and probable author of *The Protocols of the Learned Elders of Zion.*)[37]

---

35 For this judgment of Ludendorff's relation to Belarus, see Dorota Michaluk and Per Anders Rudling, "From the Grand Duchy of Lithuania to the Belarusian Democratic Republic: the Idea of Belarusian Statehood during the German Occupation of Belarusian Lands, 1915–1919," *The Journal of Belarusian Studies,* December 2014.

36 For Ludendorff's wartime rejection of anti-Semitism, see Lockenour, *Dragonslayer,* p. 57.

   For Purishkevich's outspoken post-WWI advocacy of a Russo-German reconciliation, see Kellogg, *The Russian Roots of Nazism,* p. 102. On p. 103, Kellogg reveals Purishkevich's connection to Ludendorff as a co-conspirator in planning the Kapp Putsch, which was carried out a month after Purishkevich died of typhus.

37 Steven J. Zipperstein, *Pogrom: Kishinev and the Tilt of History* (Liveright, 2018). Zipperstein's book is in large part a groundbreaking biography of Krushevan,

Later in life, by the mid-to-late 1920s, Ludendorff fell out with Hitler, at least as much because of Ludendorff's opposition to his Austrian former protégé's war aims of *Lebensraum* as on account of the NSDAP leadership's commonly given reason of Ludendorff's eccentric second wife.[38] This rejection of Hitler's Eastern policies was shared not only by Spengler, but also by virtually all the other intellectuals of the Conservative Revolutionary generation.

By "Russian," Spengler referred to even more of an archetype and less a nationality than his usages of Western nationalities. It can be

---

but contains no information on Purishkevich, other than a hostile contemporary political cartoon depicting their close association. For a solid but far from comprehensive biographical essay on Purishkevich, see Jack Langer, "Fighting the Future: The Doomed Anti-Revolutionary Crusade of Vladimir Purishkevich," *Russian Revolution Review,* 19 (2006), pp. 37–62. Among other omissions and oversights, Langer seems unaware of Purishkevich's outspoken but influential post-Brest-Litovsk reversion to his pre-WWI Germanophile views, as documented by Kellogg.

38 General Ludendorff's Eastern sympathies are partially documented in Kellogg's *The Russian Roots of Nazism* and Lockenour's *Dragonslayer.* Lockenour reveals that Ludendorff had learned the Russian language before the First World War, but Lockenour's otherwise comprehensive biography neglects Ludendorff's early Weimar-era Russian connections. Those are lucidly explored in Kellogg's book, which mistakenly describes him as "von Ludendorff," but nonetheless constitutes a crucial contribution to Ludendorff scholarship. Ludendorff's 1931 publication *The Coming War* portrays Hitler's bellicose war aims in the East as threatening to lead Germany to ruin in the service of secret societies and other "supernatural powers." Even Ludendorff's Third-Reich-era work of 1935, *Der totale Krieg (The Total War),* contains invocations of German racial solidarity with the Russians. As extreme as that book's contributions to military theory may seem, Ludendorff always insisted that his intense theories of total war applied only to what he considered defensive strategies, not to what he recognized as wars of naked aggression.

As for the somewhat overrated factor of Ludendorff's second wife Mathilde in his eventual falling out with the NSDAP, one must remember that the high position of Heinrich Himmler in the Third Reich demonstrates how Hitler did not mind promoting people with outlandish ideas he himself rejected — as long as such characters were subservient to Hitler's own strategic agenda, which General Ludendorff was anything but.

read as a reference either to the entire former empire of the Tsar, or at the very least to the short-lived but impactful German sphere of influence recently conquered from the fallen Russian Empire in 1918. This broad definition of the term "Russian" would be clarified in Spengler's lecture "Russia's Double Face" in 1922.

"Russia's Double Face" continues a theme Spengler had introduced in his debut and continued in *Prussianism and Socialism*. He questions the definition of "Europe" introduced in the time of — and in large part, on account of — Peter the Great of Russia. Like the comparatively rougher civilizational sketch of Houston Stewart Chamberlain before him, Spengler's model of "the West" is at bottom concretely Germanocentric. Insofar as "European" means "Western," he hyperbolically argues, "the real Europe stops at the Vistula," and like the Russians, "Poles and Balkan Slavs are also 'Asiatics.'"

This would not be Spengler's last word on Eastern Europe. In his mature period as a philosopher of anthropology, especially in the posthumous *Early Days of World History*, Spengler would affirm his earlier hints of admiration for the Eastern European steppe world. In that work, an unfinished but lucid draft of a planned anthropologically-themed prequel to *The Decline of the West*, Spengler anticipates more recent research demonstrating the primeval Indo-European cradle to have been located mostly in the historic Scythian and present East Slavic lands.[39] Reading his mature work as a necessary supplement to *The Decline of the West* and other writings from his early period, one can reasonably ascertain that for Spengler, the Petrine definition of "European" is perhaps reasonably valid as an anthropological term, but confused, to the point of meaninglessness, as a civilizational one.

This inclination to challenge traditionally accepted definitions of "Europe" was an authentic Prussian tradition. After all, Frederick the Great had established Prussia as a force to be reckoned with by winning a German kingdom's independence from the Holy Roman

---

39 See Oswald Spengler, *Early Days of World History: Reflections on the Past,* trans. Constantin von Hoffmeister (Legend Books, 2022).

Empire. In juristic theory, if not in socioeconomic practice, the ruling class of Frederick's Prussia became an aristocracy in Frederick's
Classical-inspired sense, in place of the old Frankish arguments for
titles of nobility. Frederician Prussia was thus a vision of a German
culture independent from the Carolingian definition of "Europe." This
common rejection, along with the related commonality of opposing
Jesuit influence in Eastern Europe, was in some ways the deepest reason for Frederick's post-Seven-Years'-War alliance with Russia.

The Prussian alignment with Russia, in Frederick's time and in the
decades after his death, had even deeper ties than that. It also rested
on the achievements of a Prussian Princess and self-made Russian
Tsarina. Though only briefly mentioned and quietly praised in
Prussianism and Socialism, the career of Catherine the Great holds the
key to the political history of the orientation that attracted Spengler
and his generation.

Catherine's father had been promoted to a Field Marshal, and she
herself backed as a Grand Duchess of Russia, by Frederick the Great
himself. Born Princess Sophie Auguste Frederike von Anhalt-Zerbst,
Catherine received her more familiar name when she married into
Russia's royal family. After the death of her suspiciously murdered
husband, Peter III of Russia, who was himself of German ancestry
and related to Catherine by blood, Catherine became the Empress of
Russia.

Catherine had studied and trained herself for this position. Not
long after arriving in Moscow, recalls Catherine in her memoirs, she
had converted from Lutheranism to the Eastern Orthodox Church,
and intensively studied the Russian language at night "while everyone slept..."[40] Her memoirs also recollect having read three works on
the ancient Romans: "Plutarch's lives of illustrious men, the life of
Cicero (by Middleton), and *The Cause of the Grandeur and Decline of*

---

40   Catherine II, Empress of Russia, *The Memoirs of Catherine the Great,* trans.
Mark Cruise and Hilde Hoogenboom (New York: Modern Library, 2006), p. 10.

the Roman Republic by Montesquieu."[41] Armed with this knowledge, Catherine went on to expand Russia's status as a great power, crippling Ottoman dominance over Southeastern Europe and — together with her native Prussia — annexing much of the vanquished Polish-Lithuanian Commonwealth.

Catherine's reasons for crushing and conquering Poland by the 1890s relate to Spengler's admiration for the tradition of a Prusso-Russian understanding. Although the Polish nobility was even more elitist and exploitative than the Germanic-derived aristocracies of the Western countries, the egalitarian ideas of the Enlightenment had nevertheless made strong headway among many Polish nobles in the 18th century, to the point of threatening a revolution. In *The Peasant Prince,* historian Alex Storozynski describes one leading enemy of Catherine's Russia, who had learned his ideas from having fought for the American Revolution. Storozynski notes that Polish revolutionary aristocrat Thaddeus Kościuszko's political career included "advocating tolerance and standing up for the rights of slaves, Native Americans, women, serfs, and Jews."[42] (The latter constituency would have particularly distinguished the dreamt-of Polish revolution from its Western predecessors, as the Polish kingdom hosted the vast majority of Europe's Jewish population.)

Here we see an element of the historic Prusso-Russian relations that attracted Spengler. Refusing the prospect of a revolution on the American and French models sweeping across Eastern Europe, Catherine destroyed the Polish Commonwealth. In so doing, she ensured that the law in the formerly Polish-ruled region of Europe would be decided not by the dreams of world-improvers, but by the traditions of conquerors who were also hangmen.

Yet there was more to the tradition of Germany's Eastern orientation than only its political history that attracted Spengler's generation.

---

41   Ibid, pp. 21–22.

42   Alex Storozynski, *The Peasant Prince: Thaddeus Kosciuszk and the Age of Revolution* (St. Martin's Griffin, 2010).

For Spengler, the idea of an enigmatic German affinity with the steppe had what he would, in his mature work, characterize as a connection of a primeval nature. This, too, was a popular theme in Weimar German nationalism — and even, in spite of Hitler's own infamous anti-Slavism, in German nationalist discourse throughout the 1930s.

Germany is purely Western by civilization, but compared to other Western nations, it is closer to Eastern Europe by geography, history, and blood. The latter likeness was observed as early as 1850 in the anthropological theories of Scottish anatomist Dr. Robert Knox, infamous as the chief customer of the professional murderers William Burke and William Hare.[43] It probably contributed to the WWI-era anti-German slur "Huns" having caught on so widely, notwithstanding that term's origin in a speech by Kaiser Wilhelm II himself.

Interestingly enough, this racial affinity between Germans and Eastern Europeans would even be glorified in German race theories of the 1930s, before the Third Reich's propaganda descended into anti-Slavism with Operation Barbarossa — much to the chagrin of Spengler's admirer-turned-enemy Joseph Goebbels, and contrarily

---

43 According to Dr. Knox's 1850 theory, the great German geniuses like Goethe belong to the "Gothic" type associated with southern and central Germany, which is but a branch of the same "Danubian race" as the "Slavonic" peoples of the Balkans. Another type associated with the Germans Knox dubbed with the virtually self-explanatory alternate terms "Saxon race" and "Scandinavian race." Knox considered this race to be "nature's democrat," a quality he admired but consigned to a dim future. Conversely, Knox disliked the third major type he identified with Germany, associated with Germany's far north, but predicted a future belonging to it. The "drum-headed Pruss," in Knox's model, belongs to the same "Sarmatian race" as the Russians.

These theories were first published in the 1850 edition of Knox's book, entitled *The Races of Men: A Fragment.* The 1862 edition is called *The Races of Men: A Philosophical Enquiry Into the Influence of Race Over the Destinies of Nations.* The 1862 edition is unchanged from the earlier 1850 version, other than the addition of some illustrations, and an afterword rejecting Darwin's then-new theory of evolution by natural selection. To Darwin's theory, Knox opposed his Cuvieran theory that races neither progress nor degenerate, but rather remain the same as they always were until the day they go extinct.

to what Michael Kellogg has shown to have been the Slav-friendly and anti-Western orientation of the pre-Beer-Hall-Putsch NSDAP. Whereas Spengler's ardently historicist early work emphasizes Germany's Western civilizational character, his much more anthropologically grounded later philosophy of the 1930s would place higher importance on Germany's primeval connection with the Scythian world. *Prussianism and Socialism* and "Russia's Double Face" still belong to his historicist period, before Spengler became a historiographer and philosopher of anthropology, but his later awe of the steppe world is already apparent in both texts.

Flirtation with the Prussian tradition of Germany's Eastern orientation was a common feature of the Weimar generation of German intellectuals often loosely labeled Conservative Revolutionaries. Of the thinkers commonly associated or affiliated with this milieu, Ernst Niekisch was unusual in his actual admiration for Communism as a governing philosophy, but his Eastern orientation was widely shared by Conservative Revolutionary circles. This affinity with the Slavic world was also shared by the early NSDAP of General Ludendorff and the Baltic German Lieutenant Scheubner-Richter, before the latter was shot dead by Weimar German police in the Beer Hall Putsch of 1923.[44] (Notably, Niekisch greatly respected Ludendorff despite their political differences.)

---

44 Scheubner-Richter and his Russian connections take center stage in Kellogg's study *The Russian Roots of Nazism*. For a biographical overview of Scheubner-Richter's life, see Paul Leverkuehn, *A German Officer During the Armenian Genocide: A Biography of Max von Scheubner-Richter*, trans. Alasdair Lean (London: Garod Books Ltd., 2008). This translated biography was originally published in Germany in 1938, while the recent English preface by Jorge Vartparonian deals with Scheubner-Richter's WWI career on the Ottoman front as an outspoken critic and journalist of the Turkish atrocities against the Armenians. Also mentioned in this book is that Scheubner-Richter, who had grown up a subject of Nicholas II before fighting for Germany in the First World War, had first seen action in the fateful civil unrest of the Russian Empire in 1905.

The Eastern orientation was also shared by Dostoevsky translator Arthur Moeller van den Bruck, whose 1920 debate with Spengler was regarded as a great milestone in Conservative Revolutionary thought. Carl Schmitt was already an influence on the Conservative Revolutionaries when he was still known as a bourgeois conservative Catholic jurist, but he did not actually belong to the Conservative Revolutionary camp until after he was excommunicated from the Catholic Church over his beloved Serbian second wife in 1927; as his geopolitical orientation turned toward the tradition of a German affinity with the Eastern European world, Schmitt's thought became both more revolutionary and more traditionally German.[45] Even the most accomplished man of political action associated with Revolutionary Conservatism, Ernst von Salomon, had taken from his experience in fighting against both varieties of Communism the lesson that the national-interest-minded Russian Bolsheviks were worthier of respect than their hopelessly doctrinaire German counterparts.

For Spengler, Russian history represents a nascent high culture that has not yet passed its inception phase, paralleled in the "Faustian" West's Carolingian age and Classical antiquity's Mycenaean age. Bolshevism, which Spengler considers philosophically alien to the Russians, represents but a transitionary phase for Russia in his view. In contrast to Tolstoy, whose ideas Spengler likewise dismisses as trivial

---

45 In 2001's *The Enemy: An Intellectual Portrait of Carl Schmitt,* Gopal Balakrishnan informs us that Schmitt deplored the anti-Slavic aspects of Operation Barbarossa, because he had grown attached to his wife's native Serbian culture. On the other hand, this moral, strategic, and tactical objection to the *Lebensraum* idea should not be confused with actual Soviet sympathies; Schmitt did support the Axis Eastern European countries. Biographer Reinhard Mehring notes that Schmitt visited both Hungary and Romania during WWII. Mehring reports that in 1943, Schmitt personally met Axis Romania's deputy prime minister and minister of justice, Mihai Antonescu. See Reinhard Mehring, *Carl Schmitt: A Biography,* trans. Daniel Steuer (Cambridge: Polity Press, 2014), pp. 379–381. To Mehring's information, it may be added that Schmitt personally met Mircea Eliade in the process of writing 1942's *Land and Sea,* and discussed the book's thesis with Eliade.

and un-Russian, Dostoevsky is seen by Spengler as the herald of the young high culture. (It is noteworthy that Dostoevsky had helped coin the term "Conservative Revolutionary.")[46]

The early Weimar transition in Spengler's political thought, first established in *Prussianism and Socialism,* would come to fruition in the conclusion of *The Decline of the West.* In the second volume, Spengler argues that the inceptions of all high cultures proceed from ruling orders he characterizes as broadly "feudal." In Spengler's model, the Mycenaean and "Dark" ages of ancient Greece belong to the same kind of seminal epoch for the Classical culture as the Carolingian period of the early Middle Ages does for the Western. From this foundational feudal order proceeds a high culture's "springtime," such as Homeric Greece or the rise of the Gothic style.

Then follows the age of what Spengler calls "the victory of the State over the Estate,"[47] which meant the rise of the city-state in the Classical world, and for the West, the rise of the absolute state in the era of the Baroque style. When this stage of a high culture reaches its maturity, according to Spengler, it culminates in "a breath of autumn in the air" in which the culture's political form and artistic achievements can "neither be surpassed nor for long maintained." In this category, Spengler places the age of Frederick the Great and, in Classical antiquity, "the fine orators of the Athenian Agora."[48]

From this maturity of a high culture and its political form follows the phase "when the Culture is beginning to turn itself into the Civilization," and the culture's signature form of a "State, with its heavy demands on each individual in it, is felt by urban reason as a burden."[49] The West first witnessed this age with the French Revolution, which ushered in the "Faustian" version of what Spengler considers "the

---

46   See Kellogg, *The Russian Roots of Nazism,* p. 31.

47   Oswald Spengler, *The Decline of the West Volume II: Perspectives of World-History,* (Arktos Media Ltd., 2021), Ch. XI:IV, p. 479.

48   Spengler, *The Decline of the West Volume II,* Ch. XI:V, p. 500.

49   Spengler, *The Decline of the West Volume II,* Ch. XI:VI, p. 510.

position of every commencing Civilization" he terms "*Napoleonism.*" This phenomenon is marked by a decline in respect for the state and for the culture's unwritten idea of law, but armies remain as relevant as ever. In the Classical culture's parallel age of the rise of the Romans, "the spirit of the army was a political power on its own account, and it became a serious question how far the State was the master, and how far tool, of its army… the army had a policy of its own."[50]

Spengler argues that the final age of every high culture is marked by "the *transition from Napoleonism to Cæsarism,*" which was exemplified in the ancient Chinese civilization by the era known as the "period of the Contending States."[51] Spengler notes the significance of the Classical version of this epoch, stretching from the Punic Wars to Augustus' establishment of the Roman Empire: "While in 300 there were *Roman* armies, in 100 there were the armies of Marius and Sulla and Cæsar; and Octavian's army, which was composed of Cæsar's veterans, led its general much more than it was led by him."[52]

For Spengler, this militaristic character of a high culture's last epoch entails the destruction of the rationalism and economism that had led up to it: "*The Imperial Age, in every Culture alike, signifies the end of the politics of mind and money.* The powers of the blood, unbroken bodily forces, resume their ancient lordship… The state of being 'in form' passes from nations to bands and retinues of adventurers, self-styled Cæsars, seceding generals, barbarian kings, and whatnot — in whose eyes the population becomes in the end merely a part of the landscape."[53] According to 1922's second volume of *The Decline of the West*, the "Faustian" West is contemporarily in its "period of the Contending States," and its resultant future "Imperial Age" is not far off.

---

50 Spengler, *The Decline of the West Volume II*, Ch. XI:VI, p. 522.

51 Ibid, Ch. XI:VIII, p. 535.

52 Ibid, Ch. XI:VII, pp. 539–540.

53 Ibid, Ch. XI:IX, pp. 556 & 560.

These ideas about war itself outlasting the state greatly influenced Spengler's student and correspondent, the highly decorated WWI memoirist Ernst Jünger. Lieutenant (later Captain) Jünger was notably drawn to a point about individualism argued in *Prussianism and Socialism*. Although Spengler rejected the liberal idea of individualism, which he considered a second-rate import from the English tradition, it is important to note that he did not advocate faceless collectivism in its place. Spengler rather believed the archetypal Prussian "socialist" ethos contributed to a type of inner individual freedom. Jünger would expand upon this idea by adding the unusual influence of anarchist philosophy.

As early as 1925's *Copse 125*, Jünger was interested in incorporating anarchist-related ideas into the Prussian militarist tradition. In that book, translated into English by Basil Creighton along with *Storm of Steel* in 1929, Jünger recalls his reaction to the events of 1918. It was then, according to his account in *Copse 125*, that it occurred to Jünger that Germany's having been less accustomed than France to domestic revolutions and insurrections ultimately left the well-ordered Germany more vulnerable in the Great War.

Although their mutual association in the early 1930s sometimes leads to the ignorant conflation of their outlooks, Ernst Niekisch later accurately criticized Jünger's 1932 philosophical tract *The Worker: Dominion and Form* as closer to Georges Sorel's anarcho-syndicalism than to Marxist Communism. *Copse 125* reveals the origin of Jünger's unusual synthesis of the Prussian spirit with anarchist-affiliated ideas: Jünger's concept, which *Copse 125* traces to his wartime experience, of combined pride in his North German paternal roots and his South German maternal ones — the former associated with the Prussian military tradition, the latter with the legacy of the semi-mercenary *Landsknecht* armies of the early modern Holy Roman Empire.

With the end of the Second World War, a key motif of Conservative Revolutionary thought was criminalized by the Allied victors. What the great general of German unification, Field Marshal Count Moltke,

had called *Machtpolitik* — the politics of force — was officially outlawed. This new jurisprudence was anathema to the philosophical
system of Spengler, who had not lived to see the beginning or conclusion of the Second World War. In *Prussianism and Socialism* and later
works, Spengler had criticized the common liberal and Marxist notion of the primacy of economic power rather than that of the politics
of force.

It was logical for Spengler to hold up the Prussian tradition as
giving lie to such economistic outlooks. Prussia had still been an economically modest country when it first rose to geopolitical power in
the 18th and early 19th centuries, first under Frederick the Great and
secondly by the end of the Napoleonic Wars. Prussia's subsequent
economic strength, achieved by the innovative Krupp family of indus-
trialists and the policies of Bismarck later in the 19th century, was an
afterthought of Prussia's militarily earned geopolitical prestige — and
not the other way around. It was exactly this trajectory, so beloved
by Spengler and other German thinkers, that the conquering Allies
vilified and sought to erase from history.

In the aftermath of World War II, East Prussia, having been overrun by the Red Army, was partly given to Poland and partly annexed
to the Soviet Union proper. In both cases, the German populations of
the former East Prussia would be violently expelled. Nor was the part
of Germany occupied by the Western Allies governed benevolently.

The harsh and violent Allied occupation of Germany has been
documented in books like *Hellstorm* by Thomas Goodrich and *After
the Reich* by Giles MacDonogh. Adding insult to injury, the Allied victors criminalized not only Hitler's party, but the entire German militarist tradition and the culture associated with it. This total destruction
of a vanquished and occupied enemy state ushered in a revolution in
European jurisprudence.

That process is inseparable from what Jünger's friend Carl Schmitt,
in what the latter unsuccessfully intended to be a memorandum for
the defense at the Nuremberg Trials, identified as the conflation of

several different definitions of the term "war crimes." The first of these, explained Schmitt, refers to "[v]iolations of the rules and customs of war, which are primarily committed by members of the armed forces of a state conducting war. This concerns breaches of the so-called law *in* war... Such laws presuppose war to be permitted and legal."[54]

Schmitt found such a definition of "war crimes" to be "of a fundamentally different nature" than the second category, that of "atrocities in a specific sense, planned killings and inhuman atrocities whose victims were defenseless humans... The rawness and bestiality of these crimes transcends human comprehension."[55] Schmitt's argument was not that no such crimes were committed by the German side during the Second World War, but that the Nuremberg Trials misleadingly conflated this category with other definitions of "war crimes."

The third definition of "war crimes," which Schmitt considered an unprecedented one, "is the war of aggression, which is interpreted as a crime as such, and moreover as a crime against international law. Here, war itself is a crime, and here one is really concerned not only with a war crime but rather, more exactly, with 'the crime of war.'"[56] Unlike the previous two definitions of "war crimes," the criminalization of "war of aggression" had never been seriously applied to any previous wars. Schmitt argued that American Nuremberg prosecutor Robert Jackson intended "to use the current war criminal trials as an especially effective creative precedent for the new international crime of the war of aggression."[57] In the process, concluded Schmitt, different types of jurisprudence and different definitions of "war crimes" were confusedly and confusingly conflated at the Nuremberg Trials.

In this way, *Machtpolitik* was not only outlawed, but placed in the same legal category as wartime atrocities. In effect, the imprecisely

---

54   Carl Schmitt, *Writings on War,* trans. Timothy Nunan (Cambridge: Polity Press, 2011), p. 126.

55   Ibid, p. 127.

56   Ibid, p. 128.

57   Ibid, p. 135.

defined "war criminal" was declared an international outlaw, an "enemy of the human race," like the pirate since ancient times. But far from actually abolishing war, the international legal order created by the Allied occupiers has since often rendered the Conservative Revolutionary notions of armies beyond the state pertinent to our age of private or semi-private military forces.

Perhaps, then, the Prussian archetype has more of a universal aspect than early Spengler's anti-universalism would allow for. In his mature lecture of 1962, *Theory of the Partisan*, Carl Schmitt demonstrates the surprising Prussian origins of the kind of contemporary partisan doctrines of war associated with Communist movements and other latter-day revolutionary activities — in theory, if certainly not in practice. While early 19th-century Spain actually waged something comparable to a partisan war against Napoleon's *Grande Armée*, it was in Napoleon-held Prussia that a modern theory of partisan warfare was first conceived by Karl von Clausewitz and others. In Schmitt's estimation, Lenin was a decent scholar of Clausewitz, but Mao understood the latter's doctrines of partisan warfare better.

Without actually endorsing the political extremism of the figure of "the partisan," Schmitt argues that the true genius for partisan warfare has the redeeming feature of being "telluric." By his use of the latter term, Schmitt tied the 20th-century German geopolitical theme of a great land-bound power with lucidly written anthropological and historical arguments of his own.[58] Schmitt usually lacked the traditional German Orientalist curiosity, but his rare focus on Asia in *Theory of the Partisan* makes the statement that "telluric" German political principles are to some extent universal.

Schmitt's conception of partisan warfare is notable for its anticipation of an age of post-state wars. This theme had been foreshadowed in Schmitt's groundbreaking work on Thomas Hobbes, in which Schmitt

---

58 For these arguments, see *Land and Sea, The Nomos of the Earth,* and *Dialogues on Power and Space.* The latter book is the best overall introduction to Schmitt's entire body of work, from his early ideas to his mature ones.

had contemplated the downfall of the Hobbesian state.[59] According to Schmitt's view, shared with much of the Conservative Revolutionary generation, the modern state is in the process of dying, but war — and thus armies, in some form — can never die.

This notion of an army beyond the state would be echoed more recently in Israeli historian Martin van Creveld's theory of a "fourth generation" of modern warfare. It was in Weimar Germany that this theoretical prescience of an age of post-state war came into being. Parts of it can be seen as already prefigured as early as 1919 in Spengler's *Prussianism and Socialism*.

In sum, Spengler's political ideas, and those shared by the Conservative Revolutionary milieu, are a product of Weimar German history. With the Freikorps wars, General Ludendorff's early Weimar career, and the Organisation Consul, Prussia's Hobbesian mask was removed. The Prussian archetype's relation to the state was revealed to be closer to that of the Franconian robber baron — as embodied in the 16th century's one-handed Götz von Berlichingen, immortalized

---

59   See Carl Schmitt, *The Leviathan in the State Theory of Thomas Hobbes: Meaning and Failure of a Political Symbol,* trans. George Schwab and Erna Hilfstein (Chicago: University of Chicago Press, 2008).

This 1938 book serves as the best illustration of Schmitt's 1930s stylistic and philosophical turn to the kind of Germanism he had once rejected as a Catholic thinker in the previous decade. Notably, Schmitt's essay from the previous year, 1937's *"Totaler Feind, totaler Krieg, totaler Staat,"* (*"Total Enemy, Total War, Total State"*) cites General Ludendorff's mature book *Der totale Krieg* as a landmark work in its field. *The Leviathan in the State Theory of Thomas Hobbes* shares with the mature Ludendorff a simultaneously anti-clerical and anti-Masonic perspective. In 1923's *Roman Catholicism and Political Form,* written before Schmitt's marriage to Duška Todorović distanced him from the Catholic Church, Schmitt had once suggested the wish for Catholicism and Freemasonry to reconcile against the peril of the rising Soviet world; yet by 1938, Schmitt had adopted a much more refined variation on Ludendorff's crudely but evocatively argued call for a synthesis of anti-clerical and anti-occult critiques, and *The Leviathan in the State Theory of Thomas Hobbes* applies a similar synthesis to an analysis of the political philosophy concurrent to the Scientific Revolution.

in Goethe's debut play—than previously thought. *Prussianism and Socialism* was written early on in the course of this process, while the second volume of *The Decline of the West* was published in its later history.

It is important to note that for Spengler, the concept of a civilization's "transition from Napoleonism to Cæsarism" is not meant to evoke despair. The high culture's creative epoch may be a thing of the past, but there are still great tasks to be achieved in its Imperial phase. Spengler's call for a victory of "blood" and "the sword" over "money" implies that the fall of the state without the fall of armies can prefigure a heroic victory against the forces of plutocracy.

This concept would be expanded upon in one of Spengler's later works, in which he notes that in the time parallel to the contemporary West in his civilizational model, the equite class of ancient Rome threatened to become a professional banking class in something bordering on the modern sense. The Roman warlord Sulla, Spengler argues, saved the trajectory of Roman civilization when he violently purged the subversive equites. "After Caesar," in terms of their major relevance as a powerful class, the equites and, with them, their proto-capitalistic ethos "completely disappeared from history as a *political* element."[60] The parallel cycle of "Faustian Man," in Spengler's view, can rewardingly look to the Prussian tradition of an army with a country as having shown the way for this great civilizational task.

Narberth, Pennsylvania
December 6, 2022

---

60 Oswald Spengler, *The Hour of Decision* (Rogue Scholar Press, 2020), Section 10, p. 97.

PRUSSIANISM
AND SOCIALISM

BY OSWALD SPENGLER

TRANSLATED AND ANNOTATED BY
CONSTANTIN VON HOFFMEISTER

INTRODUCTION

THIS LITTLE PIECE has emerged from notes intended for *The Decline of the West*, namely the second volume, which were in part even the germ from which this whole philosophy developed.

The word *socialism* does not denote the deepest, but the loudest question of the time. Everyone uses it. Everyone thinks of something different. Everyone puts into this catchword of all catchwords what they love or hate, fear or desire. But no one examines the historical conditions in their narrowness and breadth. Is socialism an instinct or a system? The ultimate goal of humanity or a condition of today and tomorrow? Or is it only the demand of a single class? Is it identical with Marxism?

The mistake of all wanters is that they confuse what should be with what *will* be. How rare is the *free* view of what is becoming! I still see no one who has grasped the path of this revolution, who has seen its meaning, its duration, its end. They confuse moments with epochs, the next year with the next century, thoughts with ideas, books with people. These Marxists are strong only in denial; in the positive they are helpless. They give away at last that their master was only a critic, not a creator. He left concepts for a world of readers. His proletariat, saturated with literature, educated and held together by literature, was reality only as long as it rejected, not represented, the reality of the day. Today one suspects it — Marx was only the stepfather of socialism. There are older, stronger, deeper traits in him than his social critique. They were there without him and have continued to develop without him and against him. They are not on paper, they are in the blood. And only the blood decides the future.

But if socialism is not Marxism — what is it? Here is the answer. Today one already suspects it, but with a head full of plans, positions, goals, one does not dare to know it. One flees from decisions from the former energetic attitude to middle, outdated, milder views, even to Rousseau, to Adam Smith, to something. Already every step is directed against Marx, but at every one, one invokes him. Meanwhile, the time of programme policies are over. We late Westerners have become sceptics. Ideological systems will no longer boggle our minds. Programmes belong to the previous century. We no longer want sentences, we want ourselves.

And thus the task is set: it is to free German socialism from Marx. German socialism, because there is no other. That, too, is one of the insights that can no longer remain hidden. We Germans are socialists, even if there has never been any talk of it. The others cannot be.

I am not outlining here one of those 'reconciliations', no going back or aside, but a *destiny*. One does not escape it by closing one's eyes, denying it, fighting it, fleeing from it. These are only other ways of fulfilling it. *Ducunt volentem fata, nolentem trahunt*[1]. Old Prussian spirit and socialist spirit, which today hate each other with the hatred

---

[1]   Latin: 'Fate leads the willing and drags the unwilling.' — *Transl.*

of brothers, are one and the same. This is not taught by literature, but by the inexorable reality of history, in which the blood, the race bred by ideas that have never been tried out, the thought that has grown into a unified attitude of body and soul, passes over mere ideals, over propositions and conclusions.

I am counting on that part of our youth which is deep enough to feel, behind the common doings, the flat talk, the worthless plotting, the strong and *undefeated*, which goes its way forward in spite of everything; the youth in whom the spirit of the fathers has gathered into living forms that make them capable — even in poverty and renunciation, Roman in the pride of service, in the humility of command, demanding not rights from others but duties from themselves, all *without exception, without distinction* — of fulfilling a destiny that they feel in themselves, that they are. A wordless consciousness that integrates the individual into a whole, our most sacred and profound, a heritage of hard centuries that distinguishes us from all other peoples, us, the youngest and last of our culture.

It is to these young people that I address myself. May they understand what this imposes on their future; may they be proud that it is allowed.

THE REVOLUTION

1

History knows of no nation whose path has been more tragically shaped. In the great crises, all others fought for victory or loss; we have always fought for victory or destruction: from Kolin and Hochkirch to Jena and the Wars of Liberation, where an attempt was made on French soil to reach an understanding between Prussia's allies and Napoleon through a division of Prussia, through the desperate hour of Nikolsburg, in which Bismarck thought of suicide, and Sedan, which just averted Italy's declaration of war and thus a general offensive by the border powers, to the storm of terrible wars across the entire planet, the first blows of which have just died away. Only the state of Frederick the Great and Bismarck dared to even think of resistance.

In all these catastrophes, Germans stood against Germans. It only belongs to the surface of history that it was often tribe against tribe or prince against prince; in the depths rested that discord which every German soul harbours and which already in Gothic times, in the figures of Barbarossa and Henry the Lion at the time of Legnano, loomed large and gloomy. Who understood this? And who saw through that return of Duke Widukind in Luther? What dark urge made all those Germans fight and feel for Napoleon when he carried the English idea across the continent with French blood? What is the deepest connection between the riddle of Legnano and that of Leipzig? Why did Napoleon feel that the destruction of the small Frederician world was his most serious task — and at the bottom of his spirit an insoluble one?

The World War is, in the evening of Western culture, the great confrontation between the two Germanic ideas — ideas which, like all genuine ones, were not spoken but lived. Since its real outbreak, the outpost battle in the Balkans in 1912, it initially took the external form of a struggle between two great powers, one of which had almost no one, the other all on its side. It ended at first in the stage of trenches and rotting armies of millions. But already in this stage a new formula of unmitigated opposition was found, which at present is designated by the catchwords 'socialism' and 'capitalism' in a very shallow sense and with the overestimation of purely economic details inherited from the previous century. Behind them emerges the last great question of the soul of Faustian man.

It was at this moment that the Napoleonic enigma reappeared, unconsciously to the Germans themselves. Against this masterpiece of the state, our most genuine and own creation, so peculiar that no other nation was able to understand and imitate it, that it was hated like everything demonic and unfathomable, the English army ran against Germany.

2

For there is such a thing. What here lashed out for the fatal stroke was not necessarily a treason of cosmopolitan inclination or worse; it was an almost metaphysical will, tenacious and unselfish, often simple-minded enough, often enthusiastically and honestly patriotic, but in its very existence an ever-ready weapon for any external enemy of the practical depth of the Englishman; a fatal epitome of political desires, thoughts, forms, which in reality only an Englishman can fill, master, use; for Germans, in spite of all heavy passion and earnest willingness to sacrifice, only an occasion of dilettantish activity, in its anti-state effect destructive, poisoning, suicidal. It was the invisible English army that Napoleon had left behind on German soil since Jena.

It is this lack of a sense of fact, developed to the point of the force of fate, which, from the height of the Hohenstaufen period, when these splendid people felt themselves to be above the demands of the day, down to the provincial philistinism of the nineteenth century, which has been christened the German *Michel*[2], worked against that other instinct and forced upon it an unfolding which has shaped its external history into a dense succession of desperate catastrophes. *Michelism* is the sum of our incapacities, the fundamental displeasure with considered realities that demand service and respect, criticism at the wrong time, the need for rest at the wrong time, the pursuit of ideals instead of swift action, swift action instead of careful consideration, the 'people' as a bunch of grumblers, the people's representation as a beer table of a higher order. All this is English essence, but in German caricature. And above all, the bit of private liberty and vested

---

2   The German Michel is the popular embodiment of German clichés. One encounters him in caricatures, pictorial jokes and humorous texts. — *Transl.*

independence that one pulls out of one's pocket just when John Bull would set it aside with sure instinct.

19 July 1917 is the first act of the German Revolution. This was no mere change of leadership, but, as the brutal form displayed to the enemy in particular, the coup d'état of the English element, which seized its opportunity. It was the revolt not against the power of an incompetent one, but against power in general. Incapacity of the state leadership? Had these groups, in which there was not a statesman, only seen the splinter in the eye of those in authority? Did they have something other than a principle to use in this hour instead of the abilities they could not offer? It was not an uprising of the people who looked on, fearful, doubtful, though not without that Michel-like sympathy with everything that went against those up there, it was a revolution in the parliamentary rooms. Majority party in our country is a name for a club of two hundred members, not for the larger part of the people. Erzberger[3], as the most tactically gifted demagogue among them, great in ambushes, raids, scandals, a virtuoso in the child's game of toppling ministers, without the slightest statesmanlike talent of English parliamentarians, whose tricks he had only mastered, drew after him the swarm of the nameless, eager for a public role, whatever it might be. They were the epigones of the Biedermeier revolution of 1848, who regarded opposition as a world-view, and the epigones of

---

3　　Matthias Erzberger (1875–1921) was a prominent politician in the Catholic Centre Party. On 11 November 1918, as chief negotiator for the German delegation, he signed the armistice with the Allies in the forest of Compiègne on behalf of the Reich government and with the express consent of the Supreme Army Command. Elected to the Weimar National Assembly in 1919, his advocacy of the 'Versailles Peace Dictate', which formally ended World War One, earned him the harsh criticism of his contemporaries. As Reich Finance Minister in 1919/20, he created structures with his tax and finance reform that still exist today. During a convalescent stay in Bad Griesbach, he was murdered on 26 August 1921 by members of the right-wing secret organisation Consul. — *Transl.*

Social Democracy, who lacked the iron hand of Bebel[4], who, with his strong sense of reality, would not have tolerated this shameless spectacle, who would have demanded and achieved a dictatorship, from right or left. He would have sent this parliament packing and had the pacifists and League of Nations enthusiasts shot.

This, then, was the Storming of the Bastille of the German Revolution.

Sovereignty of party leaders is an English idea. To realise it, one would have to be an Englishman by instinct and have the whole style of English public life behind him and within him. Mirabeau thought of this. 'The time in which we live is very great; but the people are very small, and as yet I see no one with whom I wish to embark' — to repeat this proud and resigned word to him, no one had the right in 1917. Breaking the harshness of state power, no longer tolerating anything deciding above oneself without being up to decisions oneself, that was the purely negative meaning of this coup d'état: the removal of the state, its replacement by an oligarchy of subaltern party leaders, who still saw opposition as a profession and governing as arrogance, to tear down piece by piece, to drill at, to shift in front of the laughing opponent, in front of despairing spectators within, to test the new omnipotence on the most important officials like a negro king tests a rifle on his slaves, that was the new spirit, until in the black hour of the last resistance this state disappeared.

3

The coup d'état of the English opponents of the state was followed, with necessity, by the uprising of the Marxist proletariat in November 1918.

---

4   August Bebel (1840–1913) was one of the best-known politicians in the German Empire. He was one of the 'founding fathers' of German Social Democracy. As SPD (Social Democratic Party of Germany) leader, Reichstag deputy and eloquent opponent of Reich Chancellor Otto von Bismarck (1815–1898), he became a figure of identification for the working class, which was struggling for political and social rights. — Transl.

The scene was moved from the assembly hall to the street. Covered by the mutiny of the 'Home Army', the readers of the radical press broke loose, abandoned by the wiser leaders who were only half convinced of their cause. The revolution of stupidity was followed by that of meanness. It was again not the people, not even the socialist-trained masses; it was the rabble, with the literati scum at the head, who went into action. Real socialism was at the front in the last struggle or was lying in the mass graves of half of Europe, the socialism that had risen in August 1914 and was betrayed here.

It was the most senseless act in German history. It will be difficult to find anything similar in the history of other nations. A Frenchman would rightly reject the comparison with 1789 as an insult to his nation.

Was that the great German Revolution?

How flat, how vapid, how unconvincing it all was! Where one expected heroes, one found freed convicts, literati, deserters, screaming and stealing, due to lack of danger drunk with their importance, wandering about, deposing, ruling, beating, writing poetry. It is said that these figures sully every revolution. Certainly. Only that in the others the whole people burst forth with such elemental force that the yeast disappeared. Here it acted alone. The immense mass which a thought forged into unity failed to materialise.

In the Bebel party there had been something soldierly, which distinguished it from the socialism of all other countries: clashing stride of the workers' battalions, calm determination, discipline, the courage to die for something beyond. Since the more intelligent leaders of yesterday had thrown themselves into the arms of yesterday's enemy, the pre-March bourgeoisie, out of fear of the success of a cause they had represented for 40 years, out of fear of responsibility, of the moment when they should no longer attack realities but create them, the soul of the party went out. Here — for the first time! — Marxism and socialism, class theory and the overall instinct. Limited honesty was only among the Spartacists[5]. The wiser ones had lost faith in the dogma, but had not yet found the courage to break with it. And so we had the spectacle of a working class divided in its consciousness from the people by a few phrases and concepts hammered into the brain, of leaders who abandoned their banner, the led who now stumbled forward leaderless — on the horizon a book they had never read and which those in their narrowness had never understood. The victor in a revolution is never a single class — that is where 1789 was misunderstood; bourgeoisie is only a word — but, let it be said again and again, the blood, the idea that has become the body, the spirit, that drives *everyone* forward. They *called* themselves the bourgeoisie in 1789, but *every* true Frenchman was and still is a citizen. Every true German is a worker. That is part of the style of his life. The Marxists had the violence in their hands. But they voluntarily abdicated; the revolt came too late for their conviction. It was a lie.

4

Do we understand anything at all about revolution? When Bakunin wanted to crown the riot in Dresden in 1848 with a burning down of all public buildings and met with resistance, he declared, 'The Germans are too stupid for that', and went his way. The indescribable ugliness of the November days is without precedent. No powerful moment, nothing inspiring; no great man, no lasting word, no bold outrage; only pettiness, disgust, silliness. No, we are not revolutionaries. No need, no press, no party can create a *disorderly* storm with the violence of 1813, 1870, 1914. Apart from a few fools and strivers, the revolution affected everyone like a collapsing house, perhaps most profoundly

---

5   In 1918/19, the Spartakusbund, the left-wing faction of the Independent Social Democrats (USPD) under the leadership of Rosa Luxemburg and Karl Liebknecht, severed its ties with the USPD and constituted itself as the Communist Party of Germany (KPD) in the Prussian parliament. 'Spartacists' had become synonymous with radical socialists in the November Revolution. — *Transl.*

the socialist leaders themselves. It is without precedent: they suddenly had what they had been striving for for 40 years — full power — and felt it to be a misfortune. The same soldiers who had fought as heroes under the black-white-red flag for four years wanted nothing, dared nothing, achieved nothing under the red one. This revolution did not give its followers real courage, but took it away.

The classic country of Western European revolutions is France. The echo of resounding words, the rivers of blood on the pavement, *la sainte guillotine*, the desolate nights of fire, the parade death on the barricade, the orgies of frenzied masses — all this corresponds to the sadistic spirit of this race. What symbolic words and acts belong to a complete revolution come from Paris and have been poorly imitated by us. What a proletarian uprising under enemy guns looks like, they already demonstrated to us in 1871. It will not have been the only time.

The Englishman seeks to convince the enemy within of the weakness of his position. If he does not succeed, he calmly takes up his sword and revolver and forces him, without revolutionary melodrama. He cuts off his king's head because he instinctively considers this symbol necessary; for him it is a sermon without words. The Frenchman does it — out of *revanche*, for the pleasure of bloody scenes and with the witty titillation that he can just turn a king's head on it. For without human heads on spikes, aristocrats at the lantern, priests slaughtered by women, he would not be satisfied. He cares less about the outcome of the great days. The Englishman wants the end, the Frenchman the means.

What do we want? We only get caricatures of both kinds. Doctrinaires, school foxes, chatterers in the Church of St. Paul[6] and in Weimar, a little spectacle in the street, a people in the background

---

6   From 1848 to 1849, the delegates of the Frankfurt National Assembly, the first representative body for the whole of Germany, met in the Church of St. Paul, which is thus regarded as one of the symbols of the democratic movement in Germany. — *Transl.*

watching with little interest. But a *real* revolution is only that of a *whole* people, *one* outcry, *one* iron grip, *one* anger, *one* goal.

And that, this German socialist revolution, took place in 1914. It took place in legitimate and military forms. It will, in its significance hardly comprehensible to the average person, slowly overcome the repulsiveness of 1918 and classify it as a factor in its progressive development.

But nevertheless, in the popular image of history, it is not it but the November Revolution that will henceforth take precedence. One can well imagine how, in an ideal case, a proletarian revolution would have had to begin at this point. And there is revealed the overwhelming cowardice and inferiority of the element which proletarian thought found ready to defend. Even the great revolutions are decided by blood and iron. What would eminent mass leaders, what would the Independents and Jacobins have done in this situation! And the Marxists? They had the power, they could have dared anything. One great man from the depths, and the whole people would have followed him. But never has a mass movement been more miserably dragged into the mud by the wretchedness of its leaders and followers. The Jacobins were prepared to sacrifice everything else because they were sacrificing themselves: *marcher volontiers, les pieds dans le sang et dans les larmes*[7], as Saint-Just[8] put it. They fought against the majority at home and against half of Europe at the front. They swept everything away. They created armies out of nothing, they won without officers, without weapons. If their descendants of 1918 had unfurled the red flag at the front, declared a fight to the death against capital; if they

---

7   French: 'walk willingly, with feet in blood and tears'. — *Transl.*

8   Louis-Antoine de Saint-Just (1767–1794) was an influential French politician at the time of the French Revolution, especially during the Great Terror, and a close friend of Robespierre. He helped stabilise the front in the war against Prussia and Austria and was instrumental in the overthrow of the Girondists and the execution of Georges Danton. On 9 Thermidor (27 July 1794), he was overthrown, together with Robespierre and his supporters, and guillotined the next day. — *Transl.*

had gone ahead to be the first to fall, they would have carried away not only the army exhausted to death, the officers from first to last, they would also have carried away the West. At such moments, one conquers by one's own death. But they crawled away; instead of leading red armies, they placed themselves at the head of well-paid workers' councils. Instead of battles against capitalism, they won the battles against storehouses, window panes and state coffers. Instead of selling their lives, they sold their uniforms. It was cowardice that caused this revolution to fail. Now it is too late. What was neglected in the days of the armistice and the signing of the peace can never be made up for. Thus the ideal of the masses sank to a series of dirty wage extortions without anything in return; to parasitise at the expense of the rest of the people, the peasants, the officials, the intellectuals, to shout out the words *soviet system*, *dictatorship*, *republic* so often in place of lack of deeds that in two years they will have become ridiculous, so far did their courage reach. The overthrow of the princes appears as the only 'deed', although precisely the republican form of government has not the slightest thing to do with socialism.

All this proves that the 'fourth estate' — in the deepest sense a negation — cannot have a constructive effect in opposition and *as* opposition to the rest of the people. It proves, if this was the socialist revolution, that the proletariat is not its noblest bearer. Come what may, this question is irrevocably decided. The class which Bebel had bred for the decision has failed as a unit. Forever, for the lost momentum cannot be reawakened. A great passion cannot be replaced by bitterness. And the advocates of yesterday's programme may not be mistaken: they will irrevocably lose the precious part of the working class, and from leaders of a great movement they will one day have sunk to wordy heroes of suburban riots. From the sublime to the ridiculous is only one step.

5

This, then, was the great German Revolution, proclaimed, sung about, imputed to generations — a spectacle of such terrible irony that it requires the distance of decades before it becomes palpable to the German, a revolution that overturned what it wanted and now wants without knowing what.

If one looks at the three revolutions from this future height, the venerable, the grandiose, the ridiculous, one can say: the three latest peoples of the West have striven here for three ideal forms of existence. Famous catchwords characterise them: freedom, equality, commonality. They appear in the political versions of liberal parliamentarism, social democracy, authoritative socialism: apparently a new possession, in reality only the utmost pure shaping of the *unchanging* way of life of these peoples, wholly and solely their own and not communicable to anyone else.

Ancient revolutions merely represent the attempt to achieve a situation in life in which an existence at peace with itself is at all possible and bearable. Despite the passion of the external image, they are all defensive in nature. From Cleon down to Spartacus, no one thought of going beyond their own need of the moment to work for a general reorganisation of the ancient conditions of existence. The three great revolutions of the West, however, raise a *question of power: is the will of the individual to be subordinated to the will of the whole or vice versa?* And one is determined to impose one's own decision on the whole world.

The English instinct decided: power belongs to the individual. Free struggle of one against the other; triumph of the strongest: liberalism, inequality. No more state. If each fights for himself, it benefits all in the end.

The French instinct: power belongs to no one. No subordination, therefore no order. No state, but nothing: equality of all, ideal anarchism, in practice kept viable again and again (1799, 1851, 1871, 1918) by the despotism of generals or presidents.

Both are called democracy, but in very different meanings. There is no question of class struggle in the Marxist sense. The English Revolution, which produced the type of independent private citizen responsible only to himself, did not refer to estates at all, but to the state. *The state, secular and spiritual, was abolished and replaced by the privilege of insularity.* The estates still exist today, universally respected, instinctively recognised even by the working classes. The French Revolution alone is a 'class struggle', but of rank, not of economic classes. The less numerous privileged are incorporated into the uniform mass of the people, the bourgeoisie.

The German Revolution, however, emerged from a theory. The German, or more precisely Prussian, instinct was: power belongs to the whole. The individual serves it. The whole is sovereign. The king is only the first servant of his state (Frederick the Great). Everyone is given his place. It is commanded and obeyed. This is, since the 18th century, authoritative socialism, in essence illiberal and anti-democratic as far as English liberalism and French democracy are concerned. But it is also clear that the Prussian instinct is *anti-revolutionary*. To transfer the organism from the spirit of the 18th century to that of the 20th — which can be called liberal and democratic in a quite different, specifically Prussian sense — was a task for *organisers*. Radical theory, however, made a fourth estate out of a part of the people — senseless in a country of peasants and civil servants. It gave the name 'third estate' to the predominant part, which was divided into innumerable professions, and thus designated it as the object of a class struggle. It finally made the socialist idea the *privilege* of the fourth estate. Under the spell of these constructions, in November they set out to achieve what had basically been there for a long time. And since it was not recognised in the fog of slogans, it was smashed. Not only the state, *but also Bebel's party*, the masterpiece of a genuinely socialist man of facts, thoroughly martial and authoritative, and thus the incomparable weapon of the workers, when they wanted to inculcate the spirit of the new century into the state, went to ruin. That is what makes this revolution so desperately ridiculous: it set fire to its own house. What the German people had promised themselves in 1914, what they had already begun to realise slowly, without pathos, what two million men had fallen for, was denied and destroyed. And then one stood at a loss, without knowing what should now be organised to prove to oneself the existence of a progressive revolution. It was very necessary, because the workers, who had expected something quite different, looked up suspiciously, but it was not done with the daily shouting of slogans into the empty air.

6

And so the steadfastly liberal Michel set up the overthrown throne again and sat down on it. He was the good-natured heir of the fool's prank, wholeheartedly anti-socialist and therefore equally averse to the conservatives as to the Spartacists, full of fear that both might one day discover their common ground. Karl Moor in the club chair, who tolerated all interest hunters, even the most questionable, in a liberal manner, provided that the republican-parliamentary-democratic principle was preserved, that one was rich in words, moderate in action, and that boldness, determination, disciplined subordination and other signs of a consciousness of authority remained carefully removed from his proximity. He appointed as his protector the only discovery of the November days, significantly a truly genuine soldier, and now again harboured a deep distrust of the military spirit, without which the farce of Weimar would have come to a swift end.

But what was achieved here in terms of thinking, ability, attitude, dignity, is enough to judge parliamentarism in Germany forever. Under the symbol of the black-red-yellow flag, which has thus finally become ridiculous, all the follies of the Church of St. Paul were renewed, where politics had also been not an act but a chatter, a principle. The man of 1917 was at the summit: his armistice, his League of Nations, his peace, his government. Michel lifted his cap, smiling, expecting John Bull to be great, and signed, a tear in the corner of his eye, when he really was sending forward furious France as his chief executive.

In the heart of the people, Weimar is judged. One does not even laugh. The conclusion of the constitution met with absolute indifference. They had thought that parliamentarism was in its infancy, while even in England it was in rapid decline. Since opposition seemed to them to be the sign of parliamentary sovereignty — although, however, the English system presupposes strong individualities, which are divided between two age-old, mutually dependent groups, but there was no question of strong individualities in our country — they were incessant in their opposition to a government which no longer existed at all: the image of a school class when the teacher is absent. This episode is deeply significant for the fact that it was the first time that a parliamentary government had been formed.

This episode is certain of the deepest contempt in the future. 1919 is the nadir of German dignity. In the Church of St. Paul sat honest fools and doctrinaires, unworldly to the point of comical, Jean Paul[9] types; but here one sensed mischievous interests behind it. It makes no difference whether they are the duped or the ones who agreed. These parties too often confused the fatherland with advantage. We are living through a directorial period before the Thermidor. Woe betide us if we have to make up for the skipped play! It is certain that this mendacious spectacle of an unsuccessful and unfinished revolution will come to an end. Outside, a new act of world war is preparing. People live fast today. While the National Assembly, a deteriorated Reichstag, is patching together a hut from the ruins of the destroyed state, in which profiteering and usury with wages, with goods, with offices will soon be the only occupation, others are beginning to think

---

9   Jean Paul (1763–1825) was a German poet and writer. His work was received ambivalently. Many of his contemporaries celebrated the poet's work, while others, such as Goethe and Schiller, took little notice of Jean Paul. — *Transl.*

differently about the last year. They compare what is being built with what was once there. They suspect that in reality a people never has to choose between different forms of government. Only the disguise can be chosen, not the spirit, the essence, although public opinion constantly confuses the two. What one writes into a constitution is always unessential. What the general instinct gradually makes of it is what matters. The English Parliament governs according to *unwritten* laws, developed from an old practice and often very little democratic, and precisely for this reason with such great success.

7

But make no mistake: the revolution is not over. Whether senseless or not, whether failed or promisingly begun, whether the prelude to a world revolution or a mere revolt of the mob in a single country, there is a crisis afoot which, like everything organic, like a disease, takes a more or less typical course that does not tolerate interventions contrary to its meaning. Ethical words, such as *just cause* or *treason*, are worthless in the face of the fact itself. One must, as a revolutionary as well as a counter-revolutionary, be a judge of character, calculate all the factors of the moment in an ice-cold and superior manner, apply the psychological sensitivity of the old diplomacy not to the souls of diplomats and princes but to the mass soul, which is much more difficult to understand and responds much more irritably to a mistake in tact. People's leaders with little intelligence tend to possess an infallible certainty in this. Our leaders perhaps owe their lack of instinct precisely to their genuinely German thoroughness of theoretical training. It is essential to know the duration, the tempo, the oscillation, the crescendo or decrescendo of each phase. If you make a mistake, you have lost the decision. But you also have to know what you *can* decide and what you have to let run and only in the course of the work make use of larger points of view or imperceptibly bend in another direction. Revolutionaries of great style have always possessed the tactics of great generals. The mood of an hour decides the victory of an army.

The doctrinaire will gladly study the beginning of revolutions, where principles clash clearly and hard; the sceptic studies their end. It is not only more important, it is psychologically more instructive. The circumstances were never so complicated as they are today. The outbreak of the revolution was at the same time the surrender of the country to the enemy. In contrast to all other countries, this has made our emotional position towards Marxism dependent on a powerful factor of a completely different kind. Fatherland and revolution were identical in 1792; in 1919 they are opposites. Each new phase takes place under the pressure of a hostile combination. The English Revolution took place on an island; the French, thanks to their bravery in the field, kept the decisions in their hands. In the German Revolution, however, Paris, London and New York count along, not with their workers' movements, but with troops which they march when the German Revolution assumes a form they do not desire. The Marxists have willed it so and must now reckon with it. Besides the hand grenades of the Spartacus League and the machine guns of the Reichswehr[10], there is the French army of occupation and the English fleet. The heroic Bolshevik talk in the newspapers and the daily slaughter of the Western capitalists by editorials and lying telegrams are no substitute for a revolutionary front with heavy artillery. The more one preaches world revolution, the less dangerous it becomes. The very tone of this talk betrays more anger than confidence, and after all, even the Russian revolutionaries did not put cowardice before the external enemy at the top of their programme. And let it not be forgotten that the participation of many in the November Revolution did not arise out of enthusiasm for any programme, but out of despair, out of hunger, out of the tension of nerves that could no longer be borne. The Versailles resolutions allow the state of war to continue, but how long will one be allowed to cease its mental effect for rather than against Marxist

---

10   Reichswehr was the official name of the German armed forces, which were organised as a professional army during the Weimar Republic and the first years of the Third Reich, from 1921 to 1935. — *Transl.*

aims? The weapon of the general strike is worn out. The lost first year of a young movement cannot be made up for, and even the spectacle of the National Assembly may well take against the assembly, but not necessarily for the cause of its pitiful innovators. And finally, note the rapidly approaching point in time, which inwardly concludes every revolution, when the real people want peace and order at any price and can no longer be moved to take a stand on questions of principle even by the strongest pressure from the revolutionary minority. It is not in anyone's power to postpone or cancel this moment. Compare the figures of voter participation in the Jacobin referenda, which are often suppressed in socialist writings, with those at the time of the installation of the consul Bonaparte, and one realises: even the French people had finally had enough of the revolutionary state. The patience of the German people will sooner come to an end.

But, on the other hand, not only the fundamental supporters, but also the fundamental opponents of every coup are in danger of being mistaken. A deep but vague disappointment is far from the decision to renounce. The feeling of a failed uprising, as it exists today in wide strata, is like an open wound that cannot bear to be touched. What no effort on the part of the radicals would be able to do, the slightest attempt on the part of the counter-group to end the revolution by force would immediately bring about: a wild bitterness of contagious power, which can be exploited by determined leaders for far-reaching actions. The course of events would thus change decisively, not in the sense and duration, but in the form and intensity. It could become very bloody. Today we find ourselves in the midst of the movement with that unfathomable attitude of the mass soul which in the other great revolutions has also given the cleverest connoisseurs sudden surprises. Does the tense calmness conceal an unweakened will, or does the irritable noise betray an inkling of ultimate failure? Is it too late for action by the supporters? Too early for action by the opponents? It is known that things which must not even be touched at a certain time fall of their own accord two years later. That was true in 1918, but it

will be true in the opposite sense in the near future. Yesterday's court-
iers are today's regicides and today's regicides are tomorrow's dukes.
No one can vouch for the duration of his conviction in such times.

But what periods of time are to be reckoned with here? Is it
months or years? The cycle of the German Revolution, once and as
it has appeared, is fixed in terms of tempo and duration. No one may
know them, but these factors are nevertheless present in their fateful
determination. He who errs in them perishes. The Girondists[11] per-
ished in this way because they had the summit of the revolution behind them, but also Babeuf[12] because he believed it was ahead of him.
Even the intervention of new wars, even the appearance of a great
personality would change nothing. They would be able to suddenly
and completely transform the world-historical phenomenon — which,
of course, means everything to ordinary observers — but they would
only confirm the deeper meaning of the German Revolution in its essence. A great man is one who understands the spirit of his time, in
whom this spirit has become a living form. He comes, not to dissolve
it, but to fulfil it.

Where this spirit of German socialism comes from shall now be
developed.

---

11   The Girondists were a political grouping of the French Revolution that stood in
opposition to the Jacobins in the National Convention, even though they had
overthrown the king together. The name derives from the origin of their leaders from the Gironde countryside near Bordeaux. The Girondists represented
the propertied middle class of merchants and entrepreneurs and insisted on
property rights and economic freedom. They were stripped of their power by
the Jacobins in 1793/1794. Their leaders were arrested, executed or forced to
commit suicide. — *Transl.*

12   François Noël Babeuf (1760–1797) was a political journalist and agitator during the French Revolution. He is considered a disseminator of early socialist
ideas. — *Transl.*

SOCIALISM AS A WAY OF LIFE

8

Six thousand years of higher human history lie before us. Out of the mass that has spread over the whole planet, history in the deeper sense, the spectacle and destiny of the great cultures stand out. They lie before the eye of the beholder as worlds of forms of similar construction, powerful soul life that gains visible form, innermost mystery that expresses itself in living, progressing reality.

An unchanging ethos is at work in them. It not only shapes a very specific type of belief, thinking, feeling, doing, of state, art and order of life, but also an ancient, Indian, Chinese, Western type of 'human being' with a completely unique attitude of body and soul, uniform in instinct and consciousness, *race in a spiritual sense.*

Each of these entities is complete and independent in itself. Historical influences, over whose dense fabric common historiography forgets everything else, cling to the most outward; inwardly cultures remain what they are. Thus they flourish along the Nile and the Euphrates, the Ganges, the Hoangho and the Aegean Sea, in the Semitic desert and the Nordic river-rich plain, breeding the people of their landscape into peoples *who are not creators but creations of these cultures,* differing from one another in spirit and sense and passionately opposed to one another: Dorians and Ionians, Hellenes and Etrusco-Romans — the peoples of the ancient Chinese world — Teutons and Romans, Germans and English; but towards the outside and towards a foreign culture, immediately appearing as a unity: the ancient, the Chinese, the Western man.

An *idea* rests in the depths of every culture, which announces itself in meaningful primeval words: the Tao and Li of the Chinese, the Logos and the 'Being' (τò ὄν) of the Apollonian Greeks, will, power, space in the languages of Faustian man, who distinguishes himself above all others by his insatiable will for infinity, who with the telescope vanquishes the dimensions of space, with rails and wires those of the earth's surface, with his machines nature, with his historical thinking the past, which he classifies in his own existence as 'world history', with his remote weapons subjugates the whole planet together with the remnants of all older cultures, on which he now imposes his own forms of existence — for how long?

For in the end, after a measured series of centuries, every culture is transformed into civilisation. What was alive becomes rigid and cold. Inner expanses, spaces of the soul are replaced by expansion in the physically real; life in the sense of Meister Eckhart[13] becomes life in the sense of national economy; *violence of ideas becomes imperialism*. Last, very earthly ideals spread out, mature moods with the full experience of age: from Socrates, Lao Tzu, Rousseau, Buddha onwards, the path always turns downwards. They are all inwardly related, without real metaphysics, spokesmen for practical, conclusive world-views and attitudes to life, for which we have comprehensive names such as Buddhism, Stoicism, socialism.

9

And so socialism in this late sense, not as a dark primal instinct as it expresses itself in the style of Gothic cathedrals, in the ruling will of great emperors and popes, in the Spanish and English founding of empires in which the sun never sets, but as a political, social, economic instinct of realistically conceived peoples, designates a stage of our civilisation, no longer of our culture, which came to an end around 1800.

But in this instinct, now turned completely outwards, the old Faustian will to power, to the infinite, lives on in the terrible will to unconditional world domination in the military, economic, intellectual sense, in the fact of the World War and the idea of world revolution,

13   Meister Eckhart (1260–1328) was a Dominican friar in Thuringia, Germany. He was a scholastic philosopher and theologian, and the main representative of 'German mysticism'. — *Transl.*

in the determination to weld the teeming mass of humanity into a whole by the means of Faustian technology and invention. And so modern imperialism is directed at the *whole* planet. The Babylonian one had confined itself to the Near East, the Indian one to India, the ancient one found its limits in Britain, Mesopotamia and the Sahara, the Chinese one at the Caspian Sea. We know no frontier. We have made America a part of Western Europe through a new migration of peoples; we have occupied all parts of the earth with cities of our type, subjugated them to our thinking, our ways of life. It is the highest possible expression of our dynamic world feeling. What we believe, all should believe. What we want, all should want. And since life has become for us external life — political, social, economic life -, then all should submit to our political, social, economic ideal or perish.

I have called this increasingly clear consciousness modern socialism. It is what we have in common. It works in every human being from Warsaw to San Francisco; it forces each of our peoples under the spell of its creative power.

But only us. Ancient, Chinese, Russian socialism in this sense does not exist.

Within this powerful overall consciousness, however, hostility and contradiction reign. For the soul of each individual culture suffers from a *single but incurable* discord. The history of every culture is a never-ending struggle between peoples, between classes, between individuals, between the qualities of an individual — always over one and the same grave question. A sense of opposition arises as soon as a creation comes to light. Since Nietzsche, we have been familiar with the great antagonism in ancient existence, which continues to take on new forms: Apollo and Dionysus, Stoa and Epicurus, Sparta and Athens, senate and plebs, tribunate and patriciate. At Cannae, Epicurean Hellenism faced Stoic Senatorial Rome in Hannibal. At Philippi, the Spartan element of Rome succumbed to the Athenian element of the caesars. And even in Nero's matricide, the Dionysian spirit of *panem et circenses*[14] triumphed over the Apollonian severity of the Roman matron. In the Chinese world, the opposites of all epochs, in life and thought, battles and books, are linked to the names Confucius and Lao Tzu and the untranslatable concepts of Li and Tao. And likewise it is one and the same strife in the Faustian soul that in Gothic and Renaissance, Potsdam and Versailles, Kant and Rousseau, socialism and anarchism, determines our fate and will determine it until the last times.

Nevertheless, this destiny is a unity. Contradiction and opposition serve a higher reality. Epicurus is another form of the Stoa, Aeschylus has Apollo and Dionysus, Caesar has united senate and plebs. The Taoism of Lao Tzu helped create Confucian China. The Western peoples with anarchic instincts are socialist in the larger sense of Faustian reality.

THE ENGLISH AND THE PRUSSIANS

10

Three peoples of the West have embodied socialism in a great sense: the Spanish, the English and the Prussians. From Florence and Paris the anarchic antagonism formed itself in two others: the Italians and the French. The struggle between these two world feelings is the basic structure of what we call modern world history.

In the 15th century, the soul of Florence rebelled against the Gothic spirit, which, with its tremendous tendency towards the boundless, discharged itself in the figures of the great emperors and popes, the Crusades, the cathedral buildings, chivalry and the monastic orders. What we call the Renaissance, the anti-Gothic will to limited art and dainty thought, is, with the heap of robber states of all those

---

14   Latin: 'bread and circuses' (bread and games). — *Transl.*

republics and *condottieri*[15], the politics of the moment as it lives on in Macchiavelli's classic book, the narrow horizon of all power plans even of the Vatican at that time, a protest against the depth and breadth of the Faustian world consciousness. In Florence, the type of the Italian people emerged.

For the second time, the contradiction arose in the great century of France. Racine stands next to Rafael, the *esprit* of the Parisian salons next to that of the Medicean circle. The politics of the Borgia and Sforza were repeated in Louis XIV's wars of plunder, and the Renaissance ideal of the free master was repeated in '*l'état c'est moi*'[16]. French and Italians are next of kin.

But between the birth of these peoples lies the *Spanish* century, from the storming of Rome (1527), where the Spanish spirit broke the Renaissance spirit, to the Peace of the Pyrenees[17] (1659), where it gave way to the French one. Here the Gothic revives for the last time in magnificent forms. In the Castilian grandeur, chivalry comes to an end — Don Quixote, the Spanish Faust! The Jesuits were the only and last great foundation since those orders of chivalry that had arisen in the fight against the infidels. The empire of the Spanish Habsburgs realised the Hohenstaufen idea, the Council of Trent the idea of the papacy.

With the Spanish-Gothic spirit of the Baroque, a strong and austere lifestyle spread across the Western European world. The Spaniard feels a great mission within himself, not an 'I' but an 'it'. He is a soldier or a priest. He serves God or the king. It was only the Prussian style that brought an ideal of such austerity and renunciation back

---

15 *Condottieri* were leaders of mercenary troops. — *Transl.*

16 French: 'I myself am the state.' — *Transl.*

17 The Peace of the Pyrenees was the peace agreement between France and Spain on 7 November 1659, ending the Franco-Spanish War that had lasted since 1635. — *Transl.*

into existence. In Duke Alba[18], the man of great devotion to duty, we should have found kindred traits. The Spanish and Prussian people alone rose up against Napoleon. *And here, in the Escorial*[19], *the modern state was created.* The great politics of interests of dynasties and nations, cabinet diplomacy, war as a planned and calculated move in the midst of far-reaching political combinations — all this came from Madrid. Bismarck was the last *Spanish*-style statesman.

The political sense of power of Florence and Paris is satisfied in the border skirmish. Leibniz vainly proposed the conquest of Egypt to Louis XIV, Columbus vainly knocked at both places. Subdue Pisa, win the Rhine frontier, diminish the neighbour, humiliate the enemy — this has been the trajectory of political thought ever since. The Spanish spirit wants to conquer the planet, an empire where the sun never sets. Columbus entered its service; compare the Spanish conquistadors with the Italian *condottieri*. It was the Spaniards who made the whole surface of the earth the object of Western European politics. Italy itself became a Spanish province. And one can well understand the powerful opposition that brought about the storming of Rome: the Renaissance Church was put to an end there. The Spanish-Gothic style, which still dominates the Vatican today, confronted the Renaissance Church and the related Reformation churches: the idea of world domination has not been extinguished since then. From that moment on, the Italian and French popular spirit was hostile to the

---

18   Don Fernando Alvarez de Toledo y Pimentel (1507–1582), 3rd Duke of Alba, was a Spanish nobleman, general and statesman. He was in the service of Emperor and King Charles V and his son King Philip II and made a name for himself as an exceptionally successful military strategist and diplomat. In the Eighty Years' War, he led the Spanish troops and put down the Dutch rebellion so violently that he was nicknamed the 'Iron Duke'. From 1567 to 1573, he was governor of the Spanish Netherlands. — *Transl.*

19   The Royal Site of San Lorenzo de El Escorial is a palace and monastery complex built between 1563 and 1584 on the initiative of King Philip II of Spain in the town of San Lorenzo de El Escorial in the Madrid region. It is the largest Renaissance building in the world. — *Transl.*

Church, not in so far as it represented religion, but in so far as it represented the Spanish idea of universal rule. The Gallican ecclesiastical policy of the French kings, of the Revolution, of Napoleon, the anticlerical attitude of the Kingdom of Italy can be explained in this way. The Church, however, based itself on Madrid and Vienna.

For Vienna, too, is a creation of the Spanish spirit. Language alone does not create a people. Here a nation, the Austrian nation, was created by the spirit of a court, then of the clergy, then of the nobility. It has become inwardly alien to the other Germans, irrevocably, for a people of ancient breeding cannot change, even if it should temporarily delude itself about it. This people is Habsburg and Spanish, even if no one of the House of Habsburg should live any longer; may its intellect say no, its instinct affirms it. In 1648, Spanish Germany, in the shape of the imperial house, succumbed to French Germany in the shape of the individual princes, whose courts henceforth thought, acted and lived in the style of Versailles, namely particularistic and territorial, obsessed with border expansions and averse to universal plans. Wallenstein's[20] powerful plans for the march on Constantinople and the transformation of the Baltic into a Spanish naval base marked the peak, his apostasy and death the great turning point. Franco-Spanish Germany was defeated at Königgrätz[21]. But as late as 1914, Austria's declaration of war on Serbia was a diplomatic act in the Spanish cabinet style of the 16th century, while England, with

---

20 Albrecht von Wallenstein (1583–1634) was a military leader in the Thirty Years' War. He raised huge armies for the Holy Roman Emperor Ferdinand II. As a result, the emperor and the Catholics had great successes in the war. However, the emperor became afraid that Wallenstein would become too powerful and betray him, and so he had Wallenstein murdered. — *Transl.*

21 On 3 July 1866, Prussian troops defeated the armies of Austria and Saxony in the Battle of Königgrätz in what was then the Bohemian part of Austria (today Hradec Králové, Czech Republic). Prussia's victory over Austria made Prussia the leading power among the German territorial powers in the further conflicts of the fratricidal war and can indirectly be seen as paving the way for the founding of the German Empire in 1871. — *Transl.*

the tactically superior diplomatic means of the 19ᵗʰ century, did not declare but forced the World War in this form.

The English peace at Fontainebleau and the Prussian one at Hubertusburg, both in 1763, conclude the French century. With the resignation of the Romans, the management of Western European destiny by the Germanic peoples begins. The birth of the modern English people is in the 17ᵗʰ century, that of the Prussian in the 18ᵗʰ century. It is the most recent and the last. What was formed here on the Thames and the Spree from unconsumed humanity embodies the traits of the Faustian will to power and the inclination to infinity in the purest and most energetic form. Italian and French existence seem small next to it, the times of their political heights are intermediate acts in a great drama. Only the Spanish, English and Prussian spirits have given *universal ideas* to European civilisation: ultra-montanism, capitalism, socialism in a more significant sense than is associated with these words today.

And yet — with France, culture in the West has also come to an end. Paris has poured all the creations of the early Gothic period, the Italian Renaissance, the Spanish Baroque into the last, ripest, sweetest form: Rococo. There is only French culture. Civilisation begins with England. France dominates the spirit, the conviviality, the taste, England the style of practical life, the style of money.

11

I do not want to be misunderstood about the term Prussianism. Although the name refers to the landscape in which it found a powerful form and began a great development, this is true: Prussianism is an attitude to life, an instinct, an inability to be different; it is an epitome of mental, spiritual and therefore ultimately also bodily qualities which have long since become characteristics of a race, and indeed of the best and most characteristic specimens of this race. Not every Englishman by birth is an 'Englishman' in the sense of a race, and not every Prussian a 'Prussian'. In this word lies everything that we Germans possess not in vague ideas, desires, notions, but in fateful will, obligation, ability. There are genuinely Prussian natures everywhere in Germany — I'm thinking of Friedrich List[22], of Hegel[23], of many a great engineer, organiser, inventor, scholar, and above all of a type of German worker — and since Roßbach and Leuthen there have been countless Germans who possess a little bit of Prussianism deep in their souls, an ever-ready possibility that suddenly presents itself at great moments in history. But so far only the creations of Frederick William I and Frederick the Great are genuine Prussian realities: the Prussian state and the Prussian people. However, every superior reality is fruitful. In today's concept of the German, in today's type of the German, the Prussian element is already strongly invested vis-à-vis outmoded ideologies. The most valuable Germans do not even know it. With its sum total of factual sense, discipline, *esprit de corps*[24], energy, it is a promise of the future, but still threatened not only in the people, but in each individual by that jumble of dying traits that are meaningless and dangerous to Western civilisation, although often sympathetic, for which the word 'German Michel' has long since become characteristic.

22 Friedrich List (1789–1846) was an important German-American national economist. He espoused the doctrine of the independence of the national economy. To realise his goals, he called for the implementation of protective tariffs and the expansion of the railway network to improve the infrastructure. He is considered a pioneer of the German Customs Union. To this day, his ideas of creating large economic areas with a corresponding transport structure have not lost their relevance. — *Transl.*

23 Georg Wilhelm Friedrich Hegel (1770–1831) was a German philosopher. He taught the philosophy of absolute idealism. In doing so, he proceeded strictly systematically. In his 'phenomenology', he shows the development of philosophical thought up to reason. It means reflection on oneself as the consciousness of oneself. Hegel's entire work is characterised by his dialectical thinking. Karl Marx's concept of dialectical materialism — the belief that things determine ideas and ideas change because things change — was directly influenced by Hegel. — *Transl.*

24 French: sense of community within a certain group of people. — *Transl.*

For the 'German' in this idealistic sense of professors and enthusiasts is a deformity, provisionally established as a unity by a common language. He is apolitical and impractical, not a 'race' in the sense of instincts uniformly directed towards the real. A remnant of congealed inner Gothic still remains, with the tendrils and tangles of an eternally childlike soul. German Romanticism and its dreamy politics of 1848 have brought it back to the surface. But there is also a Gothic remnant, dressed up in English rags and terms, of that trivial cosmopolitanism and rapture for friendships between nations and goals of humanity, which, in serious cases, to the point of betrayal out of simplicity or ideology, sings or writes or speaks about what the Spanish sword and English money did. These are the eternal provincials, the simple-minded heroes of German first-person novels with inner development and an astonishing lack of ability to face the world, the bourgeois of all associations, beer tables and parliaments, who consider this lack of their own ability to be the fault of the state institutions with which they cannot cope. Sleepy inclination to English liberalism with its hostility to the state, which one likes to feel, while one overlooks the taut initiative of the English private citizen even in the political sphere, bourgeois inclination to Italian-French petty statehood, which has long since allowed a particularistic bourgeoisie to grow around French-style courts, which does not think beyond its border neighbour and perceives order as hostile to culture, without being able to inculcate the spirit of this culture, zeal for Spanish ecclesiastical authority — all this impractical, subaltern, stupid but honest, formless without hope of future forms, obsolete, also spiritually barren, killing, diminishing, dragging down, the inner enemy of every German for himself and of all Germans as a nation — that is Michelism, which stands beside the types of the five creative peoples as the only type of negation, testimony to a kind of Gothic humanity from which the maturing culture beyond the Renaissance and Reformation has not developed a race in the new sense.

12

The *organised* settlement of the Slavic Ostmark[25] was carried out by Germans of all tribes. But it was dominated by Lower Saxons, and so the core of the Prussian people is most closely related to the English. They are the same Saxons, Frisians and Angles who subjugated the Celtic Britons in free Viking bands, often under Norman and Danish names. What grew up along the Thames and in that sandy desert around the Havel and the Spree, which in its bleakness, grandeur and heaviness of fate has no equal except in Latium, the Roman Campagna, in those early times, still reveals the forefathers of its will today in the rigid figures of Widukind[26], Margrave Gero and Henry the Lion[27].

But there were two moral imperatives of the most opposite kind that slowly developed out of the Viking spirit and the Order spirit of the Teutonic Knights. The one carried the Germanic idea within itself, the other felt it *above* itself: *personal independence and supra-personal community*. Today they are called individualism and socialism. There are virtues of the first order that stand behind these words: personal responsibility, self-determination, resoluteness, initiative there — loyalty, discipline, selfless renunciation, self-chastisement here. To be free — and to serve: there is nothing more difficult than both of these, and peoples whose spirit, whose being is set on such abilities, who can *truly* be free or serve, may well have the courage to

---

25 The Saxon Ostmark was an area settled by Elbe Slavs east of the Elbe and Saale rivers, which had been conquered and administered by Margrave Gero on behalf of Frankish King, and later Holy Roman Emperor, Otto I from 937 to 965. — *Transl.*

26 Widukind was the leader of the Saxons and Charlemagne's main opponent and was defeated by the latter. — *Transl.*

27 Henry the Lion (1129/30–1195), from the Welf dynasty, was the duke of Bavaria and Saxony and the most powerful German imperial prince of his time. His campaigns of conquest made him so strong that he eventually became the rival of Emperor Frederick Barbarossa, who could not accept this in the long run and eventually stripped Henry of his power. — *Transl.*

pursue a great destiny. Service — that is the old Prussian style, related to the old Spanish style, which also forged a people in the chivalrous struggle against the heathen. No 'I', but a 'we', a sense of community in which everyone is absorbed with their entire being. The individual is not important; he has to sacrifice himself for the whole. Here it is not every man for himself, but all for all, with that inner freedom in a great sense, the *libertas oboedientiae*, the freedom in obedience, which has always distinguished the best specimens of Prussian breeding. The Prussian army, the Prussian civil service, Bebel's working class — these are products of that breeding thought. The other, however, has driven out into the American prairies all that had Viking blood in its veins — Englishmen, Germans, Scandinavians, a late continuation of those Greenland voyages of the Edda period which had already touched the Canadian coast around 900, an immense migration of Germanic peoples with a full longing for distance and boundless expanse, adventurous multitudes, from whom a Saxon nation emerged, but separated from the mother soil of Faustian culture and therefore without the 'inner basalts' in Goethe's phrase, with traits of the old efficiency and the old noble blood, but without roots and therefore without a future.

This is how the English and the Prussian types emerge. It is the difference between a people whose soul has developed out of the consciousness of an *insular existence* and another that guarded a march that was exposed to the enemy on all sides without natural borders. In England, *the island replaced the organised state*. A country without a state was only possible under this condition; it is the precondition of the modern English soul, which awoke to self-consciousness in the 17th century, when the Englishman became the undisputed *master* of the British Isle. In this sense, the landscape is *creative*: the English people formed themselves; the Prussian people were formed in the 18th century by the Hohenzollerns, who, coming from the south, had themselves received the spirit of the March of Brandenburg[28] land-scape, had themselves become servants of the order idea of the state.

Maximum and minimum of the supra-personal socialist idea of the state — *state and non-state*: these are England and Prussia as political realities. For the English, 'state' of liberal style is the one which is not noticed at all, which makes no claim at all on individual existence, gives it no content, serves it only as a means. No compulsory education, no compulsory military service, no compulsory insurance, this is how England went through the century between Waterloo and the World War, only to lose each of these negative rights. This hostility to the state found expression in the word *society*, which displaces *state* in the ideal sense. As *société* it enters the French Enlightenment; Montesquieu found that *'des sociétés de vingt à trente millions d'hommes — ce sont des monstres dans la nature*[29]*'*. This was a French anarchic thought in an English version. It is well known how Rousseau hid his hatred of commanding orders behind this word, and Marx, with his equally English-oriented conceptual world, followed suit. The German Enlightenment said 'society' in the sense of human society, which did not happen before Goethe, Schiller, Herder[30]. Lessing still spoke of the human race. It then became a favourite word of German liberalism, with which the 'state', demanding greatness, could be removed from one's thinking.

But England replaced the state with the concept of the free *private individual* who, alienated from the state and hostile to order, demands

---

28 The March of Brandenburg is a historical landscape in what is now eastern Germany and western Poland. — *Transl.*

29 French: 'Societies of twenty to thirty million men — these are monsters in nature.' — *Transl.*

30 Johann Gottfried Herder (1744–1803) was an important German poet, translator, theologian and philosopher of history and culture during the Weimar Classic period. He was one of the most influential thinkers of his time and, together with Christoph Martin Wieland, Johann Wolfgang von Goethe and Friedrich Schiller, is part of the 'quadrumvirate' of Weimar Classicism. He started the tradition of collecting folk tales. — *Transl.*

the ruthless struggle for existence because only in this can he bring his best, his old Viking instincts to bear. If Buckle[31], Malthus[32], Darwin later saw the basic form of society in the struggle for existence, they were absolutely right for their country and people. But England had not found this form in its high perfection, the germs of which can be found in the Icelandic sagas, but had created it. Even the band of William the Conqueror, who took England in 1066, was a society of chivalrous adventurers; it was the English trading companies that conquered and exploited whole countries, most recently, since 1890, the interior of South Africa. Finally, it was the whole nation that developed the old Nordic robber or merchant instinct towards all realities, towards property, labour, foreign peoples, the weaker specimens and classes of its own people, which finally also shaped English politics into a masterly, extremely effective weapon in the struggle for the planet. The private man is the complementary term to society; he denotes a sum of ethical, very positive qualities, which, like everything of ethical value, are not learned but are carried in the blood and slowly formed to perfection in chains of generations. After all, English politics is a politics of private men and groups of such. *That and nothing else is what parliamentary government means.* Cecil Rhodes was a private man who conquered countries; the American billionaires are private men who rule countries through a subordinate class of professional politicians. German liberalism, however, in its

---

31　Henry Thomas Buckle (1821–1862) was an English historian and a prominent chess player. — *Transl.*

32　Thomas Robert Malthus (1766–1834) was an English cleric and economist. In *An Essay on the Principle of Population* (1798), he postulates a decreasing marginal product of labour in agriculture and that the population has a natural tendency to increase so much that the marginal product of labour falls below the level required for subsistence. The increased population thus becomes more susceptible to subsistence crises (famines, epidemics, etc.), which reduce the population again (so-called 'positive checks'). This correlation can only be broken if population growth is slowed down by moral inhibitors (sexual abstinence and late marriage as 'preventive checks'). — *Transl.*

moral worthlessness, merely says no to the state, without the ability to justify it by an equally magnanimous and energetic *yes.*

Only socialism in any version can be of inner rank in Germany. Liberalism is a thing for fools. It wheedles what it does not possess. This is just how we are; we cannot be Englishmen, only caricatures of Englishmen — and we have been that often enough. Every man for himself: that is English; all for all: that is Prussian. But liberalism means: the state for itself, every man for himself. That is a formula that *cannot* be lived by unless one says the one thing in a liberal way and does not want the other and does not do it, but finally lets it happen.

There are principles in Germany that are hated and discredited, but the only thing that is despicable on German soil is liberalism, which has always represented barrenness, the failure to understand what was necessary at the time and which, after twenty years, when it had not been possible to spoil it, was raised to the skies, the inability to cooperate or to renounce, the entirely negative criticism as an expression not of a *powerful desire to be different* — as practised by the socialists of Bebel's time — but merely of a dislike. Not fit to live, but only with a lively attitude, without inner discipline, without depth of living being, without an inkling of the taut activity and purposefulness of English liberalism, it was always only the stone in our path.

Since Napoleon it has conquered the minds of the educated of Germany; the educated bourgeois, the philistine of education, and the impractical scholar, to whom abstract knowledge has obstructed the world, have always been its most grateful defenders. Mommsen, who dominated his immense field with Prussian energy, who understood and admired the Prussian traits in Romanism, nevertheless only succeeded in uncomprehending opposition to Bismarck in parliament. Compare with him the English author of *The History of Greece*, Grote, a banker and liberal. With the fertility of field mice, our writers and professors have populated Germany with books and systems in which the English slogans of the free state, the free citizen, the free personality, the sovereign people, general, free and constantly advancing humanity have been raised from the reality of English offices into the German clouds. One must hear Bismarck, whom Bruno Bauer had already described as a socialist imperialist in 1880, speak of these educated people who confused the world with their reading. But even Bebel betrayed his always sure instinct when he once lambasted the academics in his party. He sensed the anti-Prussian instinct of the educated German, who secretly ate away at discipline in his state — and he was right: after his death, the 'educated' socialist broke the power of the party, allied himself with the educated liberal bourgeoisie and with them re-enacted the ideological scene of the Church of St. Paul in the court theatre at Weimar, where they held learned discussions on the problem of the constitution in professorial fashion, while Englishmen would have known how to act with or without a piece of written paper.

13

As a result of this ethic, the Englishman, completed on his island, attained a unity of external and internal attitude like no other modern people in Western Europe: the distinguished society, *ladies and gentlemen*, came into being, united by a strong sense of community, a thoroughly similar way of thinking, feeling, behaving. Since 1750, this splendid social attitude has set the tone for modern civilisation, first in France. One thinks of the Empire style, which in London, as a background to this way of life, subjected the entire environment to a nobly cultivated taste, practically chastened and measured from the Rococo, especially the masters of civilised portraiture, Gainsborough and Reynolds. It was a *communal feeling of success, of happiness, not of abandonment* like the Prussian. They were Olympians of business, returned Vikings at banquet, not knights in the field: wealth, along with ancient nobility, was the condition of belonging and position within this society, mark, goal, ideal and virtue. Only England today possesses what one might call social culture — though it does not have another, more philosophical one — a *deep* superficiality; the nation of thinkers and poets so often has only a superficial depth.

A German, a Prussian society of this kind does not and cannot exist. A society of 'I's' without the pathos of a strong, uniformity-creating attitude to life is always somewhat ridiculous. The German individualist and liberal invented the association for the club and the banquet for the evening party. There he develops the common feeling of the educated.

Instead of this, the Prussian style has bred the equally strong and deep *class consciousness*, a sense of community *not of rest but of work*, the class *as a professional community*, and indeed of the profession with the consciousness of being effective for all, for the whole, for the state: the officer, the civil servant, not least Bebel's creation, the class-conscious worker. We have a symbolism in words for this: above it is called comrade, in the middle colleague, below in exactly the same sense companion. There is a high ethic in it, not of success, but of task. Belonging is not a matter of wealth, but of rank. The captain is above the lieutenant, even if the latter is a prince or a millionaire. The French *bourgeois* of the Revolution was meant to emphasise equality, which corresponds neither to the English nor to the German sense of distance. We Germanic people differ only in the origin of these distances; the sense of distance itself is common to us. The swear word *bourgeois* in the mouth of the German worker denotes the one who, in his opinion, has no real professional work, who has a social *rank without work* — it is the English ideal seen from the perspective of the German. To English snobbery corresponds the German addiction to titles.

This common feeling of centuries has in both cases formed a magnificent unity of attitude of body and mind, a race here of the successful and there of the working. As an outward and yet not in-cidental expression, the English gentleman's costume has come into being — civilian dress in the true sense, the *uniform of the private man* —, which dominates without objection the sphere of Western

European civilisation, in which England has put on the world its
uniform, the expression of the doctrine of free trade, the ethics of
owning, of *cant*. The counterpart is the Prussian uniform, the expression not of private existence but of public service, not of the success
of life's activity but of activity itself. 'I am the first servant of my state',
said the Prussian king, whose father made the wearing of the uniform
common among princes. Is it well understood what all lies in the term
'the king's dress'? English society dress is a compulsion, stricter even
than the Prussian compulsion to wear uniform. Whoever belongs to
society will never go 'in civilian dress', that is, in violation of custom
and fashion. But the English *gentleman's* costume, in which only an
Englishman knows how to move perfectly, becomes the frock coat of
the German provincial and petty bourgeois, under which the heart
beats steadfastly for freedom and human dignity; the frock coat as a
symbol of the ideals of 1848, which the socialists who have become
liberal wear with pride today[33].

It is part of the Prussian way that the individual will is absorbed
in the will of the whole. The officer corps, the civil service, Bebel's
workers, and finally 'the' nation of 1813, 1870, 1914 feel, want, act as
a supra-personal unity. This is *not* herd feeling; there is something
infinitely strong and free in it that *no one* who does not belong understands. Prussianism is exclusive. Even in its proletarian version
it rejects the workers of other countries together with their egoistic
pseudo-socialism. Servant soul, subject mind, caste spirit — these are
words for something that is only understood in its degeneration and
then despised. No one despises genuine Prussianism; they fear it.

An Englishman will never understand — the whole world does not
understand — that a deep inner independence is connected with the
Prussian style. A system of social duties guarantees to the great-think-
ing man a sovereignty of the inner world which is incompatible with

---

33 Finally, the French, who are embarrassed by Faustian instincts, invented
    women's fashion alongside the costume of success and that of the profession.
    Business and service are replaced by *l'amour*.

a system of social rights, and that is the individualistic ideal. A state of mind like Moltke's[34] is inconceivable in England. English *practical* freedom pays for itself with the other: the Englishman is inwardly a slave, as a Puritan, as a rationalist and sensualist, as a materialist. For two hundred years he has been the creator of all doctrines that do away with inner independence, most recently of Darwinism, which makes the entire mental state causally dependent on the influence of material factors and which, in Büchner's and Haeckel's particularly flat version, has become the *Weltanschauung*[35] of the German philistine. The Englishman also belongs intellectually to 'society'. His civilian clothes also express a uniformity of *conscience*. For him there is private action, but no private thought. A uniform, theologically coloured world-view of little substance is distributed over all. It belongs to good manners like frock coat and glove. If anywhere, the expression 'herd feeling' is appropriate here.

14

The German Reformation had no inner consequences. Lutheranism was an end, not a beginning. Gothic Germanness was dying, and here it rose up for the last time in a great deed of quite personal content. Luther can only be explained by the Renaissance mood that pervaded the *visible* church at that time: that its public spirit was that of the Medicean court, that popes and cardinals had become *condottieri*, its administration a systematic plundering of the faithful, that faith itself had become a problem of form, the relationship between sin and repentance a question of taste such as the relationship between column and architrave, against which the powerful Gothic inwardness of the North revolted. The Church without this papacy, Gothic faith without

---

34 Helmuth von Moltke (1800–1891) was a Prussian field marshal. As Chief of the General Staff, he played a major role in Prussia's success in the Wars of German Unification. — *Transl.*

35 This German term denotes how someone understands and explains the world. It makes clear what a person considers important and right. — *Transl.*

the witty emphasis on mere form — it was only a faithful peasant revolt that did not at all question the innermost essence of ecclesiastical bondage; it bore the spirit of negation on its brow, whose fruitful passion could not last long. Creative and affirming only became the flourishing spirit of the Baroque, in which Catholicism also reached a peak of vitality and lust for life, when the Spanish created the Counter-Reformation and the pugnacious Jesuitism. Then, in the 17th century, the new peoples of the North set about forming their own religiosity out of the inexhaustible possibilities of Christianity. What they had in common was an austere spirit of action, very much in contrast to the idle culture of Florence and the barren self-tormenting dialectic of Pascal and the French Jansenists[36]. Revolutionary independentism arose in England, and under its impression in Swabia and Prussia that Pietism whose silent effect was tremendous precisely in the rising Prussian man. Outwardly serving, obedient, renouncing, in the soul free of the restrictions of worldly life, of that tender, profound fullness of feeling and genuine singleness of heart which we know in Queen Luise, William I, Bismarck, Moltke, Hindenburg, the type of the old Prussian officer in general, the individual possessed an almost dogma-free piety, shamefully veiled from others, which had to prove itself outwardly in dutiful *action*, not in confession.

The English independent, however, is *outwardly* free, Norman-like free. He formed a pure lay religion based on the Bible, which each individual had the right to interpret. What he did was therefore always morally right. There is absolutely no doubt about it in the Englishman's mind. Success was the expression of divine grace. The responsibility for the morality of actions was due to God, whereas the pietist attributed it to himself. It is not in the power of any man to change such convictions. What one must want, one finds confirmed everywhere. If this will has to lead to ruin, then that is unalterable fate.

---

36   Jansenism was a movement in the Catholic Church of the 17th and 18th centuries, particularly widespread in France, which invoked Augustine's doctrine of grace and was persecuted as heretical. — *Transl.*

It is admirable with what certainty the English instinct formed its own religious consciousness out of the French-formal, quite doctrinaire and bare doctrine of Calvin. The people as a community of saints, the English in particular as the chosen people, every deed justified by the fact that it could be done at all, every guilt, every brutality, even the crime on the way to success a fate decreed by God and for which he was responsible — this is how the doctrine of predestination appeared in the mind of Cromwell and his soldiers. The English people rose with this unconditional self-assurance and consciencelessness of action.

In contrast, there is something impractical and provincial about Pietism, which spread among a German-speaking population rather than being an expression of a German race. In small circles there was an intimate spirit of community; the whole of life was a *service*; this meagre piece of earthly existence in the midst of misery and toil only made sense under the spell of a greater task.

But this task had to be set, and here the tremendousness lies in the hardly conscious work of the great Hohenzollerns, the heirs of the Ostmark idea of chivalry; beneath all the stains of a stubborn aristocratic and urban egoism and behind all the royal weaknesses shines the thought of Old Prussianism, the only great thought that has since grown on German soil and which in the best Germans, even if they were heartily hostile to it, nevertheless conquered some region of the soul. While Swabian Pietism lost itself in bourgeoisie and sentimentality or gave up its best minds — like Hegel — to the North, a new man grew up here as a strong-minded bearer of this religiosity. A deep contempt for merely being rich, for luxury, for comfort, for pleasure, for 'happiness' pervades Prussianism of these centuries, a core of military and civil service spirit. All these things are without dignity to the imperative of chivalric duty. To the Englishman, however, they are gifts from God; 'comfort' is a reverently accepted proof of heavenly grace. Deeper contrasts are hardly conceivable. For the pious independent, work is the consequence of the Fall; for the Prussian, it is God's command. *Business and profession* as the two conceptions of work are here irreconcilably opposed to each other. Think deeply into the meaning and sound of these words: vocation, being called by God — work *itself* is the morally valuable thing. For the Englishman and the American, it is the *purpose* of work: success, money, wealth. Work is only the path that one may choose as comfortably and safely as possible. It is clear that a struggle for success is inevitable, but the Puritan conscience justifies any means. Whoever stands in the way will be eliminated — individuals, whole classes and peoples. God has willed it so. One understands how such ideas, when they have become life, blood, can raise a people to the highest achievements. In order to overcome the innate human inertia, the Prussian, the socialist ethic says: life is not about happiness. Do your duty by working. The English, capitalist ethic says: get rich, then you do not have to work any more. Without a doubt, there is something seductive in the last saying. It is seductive; it appeals to very popular instincts. It has been quite readily understood by the working masses of enterprising peoples. Even in the 19th century, it gave rise to the Yankee type with its irresistible practical optimism. The other is off-putting. It is for the few who may inculcate it into the commonwealth and by this impose it on the multitude. One is for a country without a state, for egoists and Viking natures with the need for constant personal combativeness, as expressed in English sport; it contains the principle of external self-determination, the right to become happy at the expense of everyone else as soon as one has the strength to do so — economic Darwinism. The other is nevertheless the *idea of socialism* in its deepest meaning: the will to power, the struggle for the happiness not of the individual but of the whole. *Frederick William I[37], and not Marx,*

---

37 Frederick William I, elector of Brandenburg and King in Prussia, (1688–1740) expected strict discipline, bravery, conscientiousness and tireless zeal for work from his subjects. Under his rule, society was extensively militarised. His political goals were the expansion of the public school system, the introduction of a tight financial administration and, in particular, the creation of a well-trained

was the first conscious socialist in this sense. It is from him, as from an exemplary personality, that this world movement emanates. Kant put it into a formula with his categorical imperative.

Hence, at the beginning of the culture of Western Europe, two great philosophical schools arose: the English school of egoism and sensualism around 1700, and the Prussian school of idealism around 1800. They express what these peoples are, as ethical, religious, political, economic entities.

In itself, a philosophy is nothing, a pile of words, a series of books. It is also neither true nor false — in itself. It is the language of life in a great head. For the Englishman, Hobbes is true when he sets up the 'selfish system' of egoism and the optimistic Whig philosophy of common utility — 'the greatest happiness of the greatest *number*' — and, on the other hand, the distinguished Shaftesbury[38] with his drawing of the gentleman, the Tory, the sovereign personality living himself out tastefully. But equally true for us is Kant with his contempt for 'happiness' and utility and his categorical imperative of duty, and Hegel with his powerful sense of reality, which places the hard fates of *states* and not the welfare of 'human society' at the centre of his historical thought. Mandeville[39], in his bee fable, declares that the egoism of the

---

standing army. The so-called 'soldier king' oriented government, legislative and administrative policy to the requirements of his army. These measures set the stage for Prussia's rise to become a major European power under his son Frederick II ('the Great'). — *Transl.*

38 Anthony Ashley Cooper, 3rd Earl of Shaftesbury, (1671–1713) was a philosopher, politician and writer of the early English Enlightenment. — *Transl.*

39 Bernard Mandeville (1670–1733) was a Dutch physician, social theorist and satirist, who lived in England and published in English. In his main work, *The Fable of the Bees: or, Private Vices, Public Benefits* (1714), he was one of the first to describe the economy as a circulatory system and put forward the provocative thesis that it was not virtue that was the real source of the common good, but vice. — *Transl.*

individual, and Fichte[40] that the duty of labour, is the driving wheel of the state. Is independence *through* wealth or *from* wealth the ultimate goal? Should we prefer Kant's categorical imperative: act as if the maxim of your actions should become a general law, to Bentham's[41]: act in such a way that you succeed?

It is again the Viking and the Teutonic Knight who live on in the difference between English and Prussian morality. What systems have grown out of both worlds of feeling, the *families* of the philosophers of both peoples, always differ in this one way. The Englishman is a utilitarian; he is even the only one of Western Europe; he is not at liberty to be otherwise, and if he seeks to deny to himself this strongest impulse of his nature, there arises what has long since become famous as *cant*, and the high school of which is found in the letters of Lord Chesterfield. The English are a nation of theologians, a consequence of the fact that their great revolution took place in predominantly religious forms, and that after the elimination of the state the common feeling retained no other than religious language. And theology suggested, already with a view to success in the personal struggle for existence and out of the very correct feeling that a conscience calmed by the biblical interpretation of often quite ambiguous actions means a strong increase in energy and certainty of purpose, that the actual goal, namely wealth, should not be named directly. If there is a similar

---

40 Johann Gottlieb Fichte (1762–1814) was a German educator and philosopher. Along with Friedrich Wilhelm Joseph Schelling and Georg Wilhelm Friedrich Hegel, he is considered the most important representative of German Idealism. — *Transl.*

41 The English philosopher and jurist Jeremy Bentham (1748–1832) is considered the founder of utilitarianism. Since studying law at Oxford, he was particularly interested in questions of legislation and criminal law. His main work, *An Introduction to the Principles of Morals and Legislation*, was originally intended as an introduction to the philosophy of law, but was later developed into an independent work on moral philosophy and was published in 1789. In 1808, together with James Mill, he founded the 'philosophic radicals', a movement that campaigned for more democracy in England through the expansion of the right to vote and secret elections, and for the reform of criminal law. — *Transl.*

struggle within the Prussian atmosphere, it is for position, for rank; in many cases it may be called striving, but the idea is that it is the will to take upon oneself a higher responsibility in the organism of the whole, because one feels equal to it.

15

Among all the peoples of Western Europe, these two alone are distinguished by a tight social structure. This is the expression of their need for the highest activity, which wants to see each individual in the place where he is needed. Such an order, which is based on an entirely unconscious and involuntary economy of forces, cannot be achieved by any personality, however ingenious, or by any will, however strong, to imitate foreign forms; it is natural and self-evident to a people and to that alone, and cannot really be imitated by any other. The whole basic moral feeling appears here; centuries are necessary to form the sense for distances of a certain kind in this clarity and at the same time to realise it. Viking spirit and the spirit of the order emerge again: the ethos of success and that of duty. *The English people are structured according to the difference between rich and poor, the Prussian according to that of command and obedience.* The meaning of class distinction is therefore quite different in the two countries. In the society of independent private individuals, the lower class is found together in the common feeling of those who *have nothing*, in the state as the stratum of those who *have nothing to say*. *Democracy means in England the possibility for everyone to become rich, in Prussia the possibility to reach every available rank: thus the individual is placed in the once and for all given stratification by his abilities and not by a tradition.* France (and therefore also Florence) has never known a class formation of this kind, natural and necessary to the national instinct, not even before 1789. Social anarchy was the rule: there were arbitrary groups of privileged persons of every kind and extent without any socially fixed relationship among themselves. Think of the judicial nobility next to the court nobility, of the abbé type, of the tax farmers, of the differences in the urban upper middle classes. The genuine French sense of equality is clearly marked in this incapacity for graduated order from time immemorial. In England, the nobility has gradually become the nobility also of wealth, in Prussia the military nobility. The French nobility never attained such unity of social significance. The English Revolution was directed against the state, i.e. against the 'Prussian' order in church and public existence, the German Revolution against the 'English' order according to rich and poor, which had invaded in the 19th century with industry and trade and had become the centre of anti-Prussian, anti-socialist tendencies. The French alone were not directed against a foreign and therefore immoral order, but against an order in general: that is democracy in the French sense.

Here, at last, the profound ethical meaning of the catchwords *capitalism* and *socialism* emerges. It is the human orders which are built on *wealth* and on *authority*, that which is achieved by the unrestrained struggle for success, and that which is achieved by legislation. That the true Englishman should take orders from one who has nothing is as intolerable to him as bowing to mere wealth is to the true Prussian. But even the class-conscious worker of the former Bebel Party obeyed the party leader out of the same certainty of instinct as an English worker respects a millionaire as a happier being visibly distinguished by God. The proletarian class struggle is incapable of touching differences so deeply rooted in the soul. The whole English working-class movement is built on the difference between the wealthy and the beggars within the working class itself. The iron discipline of a Prussian-style party of millions would not even be thought of there.

'Unequal distribution of wealth' is the genuinely English proletarian formula which Shaw is always mouthing; senseless as it sounds to us, it is true of an ideal of life which alone is worth living for the civilised Viking. So, also with regard to the great formation of this ideal in the Yankee type, we should speak of *billionaire socialism* and *civil servant socialism*. To the first belongs a man like Carnegie, who first converts a large part of all the people's wealth into private property and then spends it in a brilliant manner quite sovereignly for public purposes. His saying, 'The man who dies thus rich dies disgraced', contains a high conception of the will to power over the whole. But let us not forget the deep relationship of this *private socialism*, which in the most extreme cases is nothing but the dictatorial administration of the people's property, to the socialism of the official and organiser (who can be very poor), as it appears uniformly in Bismarck and Bebel.

Shaw today is the pinnacle of 'capitalist' socialism, for which rich and poor are still formative opposites of the economic organism. 'The greatest of evils and the worst crime is poverty' (*Major Barbara*[42]). He preaches against the 'cowardly masses who cling to the feeble prejudice that one should rather be good than rich'. The worker should try to get rich, that has also been the policy of the English trade unions from the beginning. That is why, apparently, between Owen[43] and Shaw, there was no socialism in England in the proletarian sense — it was indistinguishable in kind from the capitalism of the underclass. For us, however, the formative opposition is always commanding and obeying in a strictly disciplined community, be it state, party, labour, officer corps or civil service, of which every member is a servant without exception. *Travailler pour le roi de Prusse*[44] — that also means doing one's duty without the dirty pursuit of profit. The pay of officers and civil servants since Frederick William I has been ridiculous in comparison to the sums that would have placed one in the middle class in England. Nevertheless, people worked more diligently, more selflessly, more honestly. *Rank* was the reward in the end. And so it

---

42 *Major Barbara* is a play by George Bernard Shaw, which premiered in 1905. — Transl.

43 Robert Owen (1771–1858) was a successful Welsh entrepreneur of early industrialisation. He saw workers as living machines that needed to be carefully nurtured. The labour movement was inspired by his ideas, but they were soon swallowed up by Manchester capitalism. — *Transl.*

44 French: 'Working for the King of Prussia'. — *Transl.*

was under Bebel. This workers' state within the state did not want to get rich, but to rule. In their commanded strikes, these workers often enough fought not for a question of wages but for a question of power, for a world-view that was supposedly or actually opposed to that of their breadwinners, for a moral principle, whereby the lost battle was basically still a moral victory. To English workers such a thing is quite incomprehensible. They were not poor, and in their strikes they still received the hundreds of thousands which the poor German worker evaded in the opinion that it was the same thing over there. The November Revolution was therefore a refusal of obedience in the army *and at the same time* in the workers' party. The sudden transformation of the disciplined workers' movement into a wild wage policy of individual groups without mutual consideration was a victory of the English principle. The failure expressed itself in the fact that a new organism of internal discipline arose in the Reichswehr. The only capable man who appeared was a soldier. The German Revolution will continue in such military-authoritative successes and failures.

16

The same contrast, however, also dominates the *economic thinking* of both peoples. It is a fatal mistake of national economy that it talks, in an entirely materialistic way and without the slightest eye for the multiplicity of economic instincts and their power of expression, about the economic stages of 'mankind', 'the' modern age, 'the' present. It carries with it all the weaknesses of its English origin, for it is, as a science, a product of the modern Englishman with all his sense of self and lack of psychology, his only 'philosophy', which corresponds to his sense of struggle, success and possession and with which he has planted his purely English view of economic practice in all the minds of the continent since the 18th century.

From the world-feeling of the genuine settler of the frontier marsh, the colonising order, the *economic authority of the state* arose as a necessary principle. The individual receives his economic *task* from fate, from God, from the state, from his own talent — these are all words for the same *fact*. The rights and duties of producing and using goods are equally distributed. The goal is not the enrichment of individuals or of each individual, but the flourishing of the whole. This is how Frederick William I and his successors colonised the swamplands of the East. They regarded this as a mission. God had given them a task. It was along these lines that the German worker's sense of reality moved with full determination. Only Marx's theories prevented him from recognising the close kinship between his and the old Prussian will.

The buccaneer instinct of the island people understands economic life quite differently. There it is a matter of struggle and booty, and the booty of individuals. The Norman state, with its refined technique of collecting money, was based entirely on the principle of booty. The feudal system was inserted into it in a magnificent way as a means. The barons had to exploit the piece of land allotted to them, the duke demanded his share from them. The ultimate end was wealth. God had given it to the daring. It is from the practice of these settled pirates that the modern accounting system originates. From the accounting chamber of Robert the Devil of Normandy[45] (d. 1035) come the words *cheque, account, control, receipt, record,* and the present name of the English Exchequer. When England was conquered from here in 1066, the tribal Saxons were exploited in exactly the same way by the Norman barons. Never did their descendants learn to look at the world differently. This style is still worn today by every English trading company and every American trust. The creation of *individual* fortunes, of *private* wealth, the suppression of private competition, the exploitation of the public by advertising, by price policy, by stimulating needs, by controlling the relation of supply and demand, is the

---

45 Robert I (1000–1035) was the duke of Normandy and the father of William the Conqueror. According to medieval legend he was a tyrant. He subdued the nobility, made a pilgrimage to Jerusalem and died at Nicaea on his return. — *Transl.*

aim, not the systematic raising of the national wealth as a unit. When an Englishman speaks of national wealth, he means the number of millionaires. 'Nothing is more foreign to English feeling than solidarity' (Friedrich Engels). Even in recreation, the Englishman still sees an activity of *very personal, above all physical* superiority. He does sport for the sake of the record and has a sense for the boxing match related to his economic habits, which is inwardly quite alien to German gymnasts.

It follows *that English economic life is in fact identical with trade,* trade in so far as it represents the cultivated form of robbery. In the face of this instinct, everything becomes a prey, a commodity to be enriched by. The whole English machine industry was created in the interests of trade. It served the procurement of cheap goods. When English agriculture set a limit to wage cuts through its prices, it was sacrificed to trade. The whole struggle between entrepreneur and worker in English industry in 1850 is over the commodity 'labour', which the one wants to capture cheaply, the other to negotiate expensively. All that Marx says with angry admiration of the achievements of 'capitalist society' is of the English and not of a general human economic instinct.

The sovereign term *free trade* belongs in a Viking economy. The Prussian and therefore socialist word would be state regulation of the exchange of goods. This relegates trade in the economy as a whole from a dominant to a servant role. One understands Adam Smith with his hatred of the state and 'that insidious and crafty animal, vulgarly called a statesman or politician'. Indeed, to the real trader they must seem like the policeman to the burglar or a cruiser to a corsair ship.

But the overestimation of the amount of capital for economic prosperity is also characteristic of his work. That psychologically and therefore also practically — for practical life *is* the expression of mental conditions — the English concept of capital from the merchant's point of view is something quite different from the French concept of pensioner and the Prussian concept of administration is something that a materialist does not see. The English have never been psychologists. What they thought, they took for thought necessities of 'mankind'. The whole of modern national economy is based on the fundamental error of equating the meaning of economic life everywhere in the world with merchant interest in English terms, even where the Manchester doctrine is rejected in its wording; Marxism, as a pure negation of this doctrine, has completely adopted its scheme. This explains the tremendous fiasco of all predictions for the outbreak of the World War, which had been unanimously prophesied to bring about the collapse of the world economy during a few months.

Only *English*-style capitalism is the counterpart of Marxist-style socialism. The Prussian idea of *managing* economic life from a supra-personal point of view had involuntarily transformed German capitalism into socialist forms in the sense of a *state order* since the protective tariff legislation of 1879. The great syndicates were economic states within the state as a whole, 'the first systematic and generously carried out and thereby quite unconsciously developed practical attempt of capitalist society to get behind the secrets of its own production and to master the social laws, to whose unknown natural violence one had until then had to blindly submit' (Lensch[46], *Drei Jahre Weltrevolution*[47]).

German liberalism, German Englishness, however, pays homage not only to free human dignity but also to free trade. Here the comedy of its appearance reaches its peak. As long as it 'steadfastly' rejected the authoritative state, the supra-personal will, the position of the individual ego under the total ego in favour of misunderstood Viking instincts, it was metaphysical. This was the attitude of the German 'educated' people without practical talent — the professor, the thinker and poet, all those who write instead of acting. They would neither have understood nor recognised as moral the other liberalism:

46 Paul Lensch (1873–1926) was a German journalist, university professor and a member of the Reichstag for the SPD. — *Transl.*

47 'Three Years of World Revolution'. — *Transl.*

the robber principle of free trade, which includes a philosophy of the struggle of all against all. The connection between the autonomous ego in their abstract systems and that in the offices of the great trading houses was beyond their comprehension. And so German stock market liberalism has quietly harnessed the German professor to its chariot. It sends him into the assemblies to speak and to listen; it puts him into the editorial offices where he writes the most thorough articles with a philosophical spirit in order to instil the commercially desirable political convictions into the nation of readers, who have long since transferred their unlimited faith from the Bible to the newspaper; it sends him into parliament and makes him say no and yes there in order to draw ever new possibilities of racketeering from economic life in defiance of all theories and constitutions. He has made the press of Germany, which is now even considered, almost without exception, the whole mass of the educated, the whole liberal party, his business organs. The professor does not notice. In England the liberal is of one piece, ethically *and therefore* free in business, and well aware of the connection. In Germany there are always two, the moral liberal and the business liberal personality, one of whom thinks and the other directs, and only the second is smilingly aware of the mutual relationship.

Thus, today, two great economic principles confront each other. The Viking has become the free trader, the knight the administrative official. There is no reconciliation between the two, and since they both, as Teutons and Faustian men of the highest order, recognise no limits to their will and will only believe themselves to have reached their goal when the whole world is subjugated to their idea, there will be war until one of them has finally triumphed. Shall the world economy be a world exploitation or a world organisation? Shall the caesars of this future empire be billionaires or world officials; shall the population of the earth, so long as this empire of Faustian civilisation holds together, be the object of the policy of trusts or of men, as indicated at the end of the second Faust? For it is the fate of the world that is at stake. The economic ideas of the French were as territorially limited as those of the Renaissance man. In this respect, the mercantile system under Louis XIV and Turgot's[48] school of physiocrats at the time of the Enlightenment are in no way different from the socialist plans of Fourier[49], who wanted to break 'society' down into the small economic bodies of his phalansteries, as can still be found in Zola's last novels. A world economy is one of the innermost necessities only of the three genuinely Faustian peoples. The chivalrous Spaniards aspired to it by incorporating the New World into their empire. As true soldiers, they did not think about the theory of their economic expansion, but through the geographical and political widening of their horizon, they also gave the *economic horizon* of Western man the dimensions that made such thoughts possible in the first place. The English were the first to write under the name of national economy the theory of *their* exploitative world economy. As merchants they were clever enough to know the power of the pen over the people of the most book-believing of all cultures. They persuaded them that the interests of their pirate people were those of humanity. They wrapped the idea of free trade in that of freedom. This practical wisdom was lacking in the third and last, again a genuinely soldierly people. What Prussia realised in its circle was elevated to socialism through the mediation of unworldly German philosophy. But the true creators did not recognise their creature in this form and a bitter struggle arose between two supposed opponents, one of whom possessed the practice, the other the theory. Today, finally, it is time to recognise each

---

48 Anne Robert Jacques Turgot (1727–1781) was a French statesman and economist of the Enlightenment. — *Transl.*

49 Charles Fourier (1772–1837) was a French social theorist and a representative
of early socialism. He predicted that everything — including the climate, and
the animal and plant world — would change if women and men lived equally in
decentralised democratic settlements, freely followed their inclinations and let
their children grow up without coercion. While Marx and Engels rejected these
plans as utopian, other philosophers saw them as anticipations of feminism,
ecological socialism and a holistic understanding of nature. — *Transl.*

other and the common task. Should the world be governed socialistically or capitalistically? This question cannot be decided between two
peoples. Today it has penetrated into the interior of each individual
people. When the weapons rest between states, they will be raised in
civil war. Today there is an English and a Prussian economic party in
every country. And when the classes and strata have grown tired of
war, individual master-men will carry it on in the name of the idea.
In the great decisions of the ancient world between the Apollonian
and the Dionysian idea, the Peloponnesian War passed from the war
between Sparta and Athens into the struggle between the oligarchy
and the demos of all the individual cities. What was fought out at
Philippi and Aktium flooded the forum of Rome with blood in the
Gracian period. In the Chinese world, the corresponding war between the Tsin and Tsu empires, between the Tao and Li world-views,
lasted for a century. In the Egyptian world, tremendous events of the
same kind hide behind the enigma of the Hyksos period, the reign of
Eastern barbarians. Had they been called or did they come because
the Egyptians had exhausted themselves to the point of impotence in
internal wars? Will the West give the Russians the same role? Let our
trivial peace enthusiasts talk of reconciling nations: the *ideas* will not
reconcile them; the Viking spirit and the Order spirit will lead their
struggle to an end, even if the world emerges tired and broken from
the bloodstreams of this century.

17

With this, however, the Anglo-Prussian opposition enters the
realm of *political* forms. They are the highest and most powerful of
historical existence. *World history is the history of states. The history
of states is the history of wars.* Ideas, when they push for a decision,
disguise themselves in political units, in states, in peoples, in parties.
They want to be fought with weapons, not with words. Economic
struggles become struggles between states or within states. Religions
constitute themselves as states, like Judaism and Islam, Huguenots

and Mormons, when their existence or victory is at stake. Everything that has become man and human creation from innermost soulhood sacrifices man. Ideas that have become blood demand blood. War is the eternal form of higher human existence, and states exist for the sake of war; they are an expression of the readiness for war. And even if a weary and de-souled humanity were to renounce wars and states, like the ancient man of the latest centuries, the Indian and Chinese of today, from a wager of wars himself he would only become the object for which and with which wars are waged by others. If even Faustian world peace were achieved, master-men of the ilk of late Roman, late Chinese, late Egyptian caesars would fight over this empire as prey, if its final form were a capitalist one, and for the first rank in it, if it were to become a socialist one.

But to a political form belongs the people who created it, who carry it in their blood, who *alone* are able to realise it. Political forms in themselves are empty concepts. Anyone can repeat them. But no one can live them, no one can fill them with true reality. In the political sphere, too, there is no choice; each culture and each individual people of a culture conducts its business and fulfils its destiny in forms that are born with it and are unchangeable in essence. A philosophical quarrel about 'monarchy' or 'republic' is a quibble about words. There is no such thing as the monarchical form of government in itself, just as there is no such thing as the cloud form in itself. An ancient and a Western European 'republic' are incomparable things. When in a great crisis, the ultimate meaning of which is always quite different from the change of the form of government, the republic or monarchy is proclaimed, it is simply a call, a name, the cue of a melodramatic scene, the only thing, however, that most people understand about an epoch and are able to enthuse about. In reality, after such ecstasies, a people returns to the form, namely to its own, for the essence of which there is almost never a popular name. The instinct of an unconsumed race is so strong that it very soon works in its own peculiar way with every form of government which historical chance throws in its way, without anyone becoming aware that all that remains of the form is the name. It is never the constitutions in their wording but the unwritten and unconscious rules according to which they are used that may be called the real form of government. Without the relation to a very definite people, 'republic', 'parliamentarism', 'democracy' are mere figures of speech.

Thus the 'parliamentary form of government' is a specifically English growth, and without the entire prerequisites of the English Viking character, without the insularity and a development of several hundred years which has completely welded the ethical style of this people to this style of management, it can neither be lived up to nor imitated in its methods with any prospect of even remotely equal success. Parliamentarism in Germany is nonsense or treason. England has rendered impotent all the states to which she handed the poison of her own form as a medicine. Conversely, England would lose the capacity for successful politics as soon as the final development of the Western civilisation, which today dominates the globe, should lead to the impossibility of this form of government. English socialism would be betraying England if it abolished it. It is a free society of private individuals to whom, as I have said, insularity has given the possibility of abolishing the actual state and of maintaining this formal condition of their political existence until 1916 by means of a fleet with hired crews and an endless series of wars waged for payment by foreign states and peoples. This stateless parliamentarism presupposes a fixed system of two parties whose relation to each other, whose organisation, practice, interests, whose mood, custom, spirit are precisely these and no others. What we call English parties — the word means something different in every country — are originally groups of the Old English nobility, which in the revolutions of 1642 and especially 1688 separated themselves by the Anglican and Puritan confessions, in depth therefore by a certain difference in their ethical imperatives. Of the characteristics of that old Norse seafaring race to which the Icelandic sagas bear witness, the pride in noble blood, the aristocratic sense of all that is inherited and legitimate, of landed property, of war-like ventures and bloody decisions predominated among the Tories; among the Whigs the delight in robbery and plunder, in easy success and rich movable booty, in cunning and daring more than in physical strength. The types of the English imperialist and free trader have been brought up to their present form by the ever sharper expression of these feelings of life, by the ever purer breeding of the actual ruling class. That the democratisation of England in the nineteenth century was only an apparent one, and that the people were actually led, as in Prussia, by a high-quality minority distinguished by the wholeness and unbrokenness of its practical qualities, has maintained the height not only of will but of ability until the outcome of the last war.

For it belongs to the innermost essence of this policy that it is a pure business policy in the pirate sense, whether the Tories or the Whigs happen to be in the lead. The fact that both are first and foremost gentlemen, members of the same distinguished society with its admirable unity of attitude to life, makes it possible that, in spite of the sometimes bitter opposition, the great matters are settled in private conversation and private correspondence, so that many things are done which may only be conceded when success justifies the means, and which in any other country of the world would be spoiled in the din of uncomprehending and principled popular representations. The English party leader also conducts the business of the country as a private citizen. If his political ventures succeed, it was 'England' that adopted these policies. If, though successful, they lead to practically or morally embarrassing consequences, he resigns and the country rebukes him with Puritan severity for his private conduct, the consequences of which are repudiated by the resignation; but God is thanked for the grace he has shown England by the successful act itself. This is only possible when both parties are without difference of opinion in essential interests. It is true that the Tories overthrew Napoleon and took him to St. Helena after he had spread the ideas of the Whigs over the continent, but Fox was by no means an unconditional opponent of war with him. And when Robert Peel[50] finally led the Cobden[51] free trade system to victory in 1851, thus preferring the economic subjugation of the world to its transformation into a military protectorate, the Tories certainly found and recognised part of their principles in the Whigs' system. Tory policy under Edward VII prompted the World War, but the Whigs, opponents of war, tacitly prepared themselves for that possibility by welcoming 'liberal imperialists'. All this is 'parliamentarism', and not those worthless and ineffective externals which are taken for it in Germany today, such as the distribution of ministerial portfolios among party leaders or the exposure of parliamentary technique to the widest public. The latest resolutions of the party leaders are a secret even to the majority of the members of parliament. The visible proceedings are *fable convenue*[52], and the exemplary tact of both parties ensures that the appearance of self-government of the people is maintained all the more embarrassingly, the less this concept actually means. That parties, especially English parties, are parts of the people is amateurish nonsense. In reality, except in states the size of a few villages, there can be no such thing as popular government, government by the people. Only hopelessly liberal Germans believe in it. Wherever English forms of government have penetrated, government is in the hands of a very few men who rule within a party by their experience, superior will and tactical dexterity, and do so with dictatorial authority.

This raises the question of the relationship between the people and the party, or what elections actually mean in today's Western world of states. Who votes and what do they vote for? The meaning of the

---

50 Sir Robert Peel was an English politician, Prime Minister (1834–1835, 1841–1846) and Home Secretary (1822–1830), who founded the Metropolitan Police London, the world's first official police force (with the 'Bobbies' named after him), and is considered the founder of the Conservative Party. — *Transl.*

51 Richard Cobden (1804–1865) was a British entrepreneur and the leading figure of Manchester Liberalism and the free trade movement. — *Transl.*

52 French: a 'made-up story' that is considered to be true. — *Transl.*

English system is that the people elect *the party* and not an agent of their will more or less suggested by the party leadership itself. The parties are firmly constituted, very ancient societies, which are concerned with conducting the political affairs of the society of the English people in general. The individual Englishman, sensing well the expediency of this arrangement, supports from election to election the one whose intentions for the next few years are most in accordance with his own opinions and interests. He knows perfectly well how indifferent the person of the member of parliament, whom the party appoints quite sovereignly, is to this. The word 'votes' is certainly more appropriate to the average member of parliament than to his or her voters. It is significant that the workers very often voted for a businessman put up by one of the old parties instead of for the workers' candidate. According to their sober assessment of the situation, this was more advantageous for the moment. In America, where already the true Englishman is no longer behind the system, the custom has developed of the parties presenting one programme to the electors and another to the trusts which pay them, one of which is destined to be published and the other to be held. This finally touches on the decisive question *of the form in which political work is paid for in countries governed by parliament*. The naive enthusiasts for democratic conditions do not notice that today, when all peoples are guided, with or without knowledge and will, by a policy of interests, it is not the spirit of the constitutions that depends on this, but the much more important spirit of their actual application. In their harmlessness, they may be thinking of the level of parliamentary salaries. But the question is different. The monarchs of the Baroque era disposed of state revenues as they saw fit. The modern parties only administer them. And here it is merely a question of expediency whether the representatives of the great economic interests secure for themselves the electors, the MPs or the party leaderships. The first corresponds to the forms of English parliamentarism and was practised on a large scale in the 18th century as vote buying. Today, when Tories and Whigs from distinguished

classes with sharply defined world-views have become purely business representations, differing from case to case really only in their
view of the most advantageous form and the moral justification of
an enterprise, this means has become superfluous: the interests have
united with the democratised parties. In anarchic France, where clubs
and personal groups of rapidly changing number and strength appear
under the name of parties, the payment of deputies in finer or more
immediate forms is the rule. The socialist material of deputies is as
much at the disposal of the plutocracy as the rest, and the career of a
French parliamentarian is often enough taken up in the certainty that
after a few years one can buy a château. In Germany, where the parties
present themselves to the people with ideological programmes, the
stock exchange has put liberalism and heavy industry national liberalism at their service. They pay for the agitation and — partly in the
form of supplying business advertisements — the press. If the Weimar
constitution were to remain in force for even a few years, seats in
parliament would be up for grabs at a fixed price in the interests of
certain parties. The beginnings of this were already clearly present in
the first elections.

That democracy and universal suffrage are tried and tested
methods of capitalism has been proved by all countries which have
adopted these forms from England. If the liberal professor hails the
constitution of Weimar as the fulfilment of his dreams, business liberalism hails it as the most convenient and perhaps cheapest method of
subordinating politics to the counting house, the state to profiteering.

All this marks the domination of the Viking spirit over Western
civilisation, which has hitherto been thoroughly English civilisation. The form in which the *untransferable* English parliamentarism
imposed itself on the mainland and finally on the whole world is the
'constitution', by which criticism of existing governments is made an
organic part of government itself. But the *stateless* character of government, which English society developed out of itself, here passed
into the *anti-state* character of all constitutions in which a foreign, the

English principle, was contained. Thus party surrogates became necessary everywhere, which imitated the English style, which had made
the executive power a constituent part of party sovereignty, without
its content, and an opposition which, with continual friction between
the supreme power and the party principle, or between the parties because of their very different conception of party sovereignty, had not
an organically promoting but a destructive effect. Mirabeau, the wis-
est head of France at the moment it succumbed to the Viking ideas,
would certainly have returned to absolutism if he had lived longer,
in order to save his country from the pseudo-parliamentarism of the
sovereign clubs. The word *intrigue* gives exhaustively the spirit which
the anarchic Frenchman introduces into every kind of government in
place of the planned tactics of the Englishman, in order to make it
conform to his way of life. As a result, it is always *accidental despotism
as the most practically useful form of this anarchy* in which French history has from time to time reached surprising but fleeting heights of
success. This was already true of Mazarin[53] and Richelieu; this has been
the secret ultimate goal of every political club, however small, since
1789, and this has finally found its classic expression in the dictatorship of a foreign soldier, Napoleon. Macchiavelli had hoped for something very similar for the confusion of Cesare Borgia's Renaissance
politics. France and Italy alone did not produce a political idea. Louis
XIV's state is an isolated case like Napoleon's empire, not a system
of permanence, and the absolute monarchy of the Baroque as an organic and evolving form is Habsburg, not Bourbon, in origin. From
Philip II to Metternich, Habsburg has been exemplary for the *mode
of government* of almost all courts and cabinets; the court of the Sun
King had an effect only on the ceremonial and costume. Napoleon's
Renaissance-like appearance is proof of this. Only in Florence and

---

53   Cardinal Jules Mazarin (1602–1661) was one of the most important French
     statesmen of the 17th century. Together with Queen Anne of Austria (1601–
     1666), he not only determined the education of the still minor King Louis XIV
     for a long time, but also French politics. — *Transl.*

Paris could a successful military leader play such an untraditional role and set up a state of such fantastic and ephemeral forms. There was no typical form of state here. Rousseau, the theorist of political anarchy, drew the concept of his social contract from the fact of the English society, which was firmly founded in itself and worked politically with full instinctive certainty, which in the end nevertheless demanded dictatorship as an occasional and accidental rescue from the motley of all individual wills. In England, Napoleon could have become prime minister in the event of a revolution, in Prussia field marshal, in Spain both, and with unlimited authority. In Charlemagne's costume, he is only conceivable in France and Italy.

In Prussia there was now a real state in the most sophisticated meaning of the word. Here, strictly speaking, there was no private citizen. Everyone who lived within the system, which worked with the exactness of a good machine, belonged to it somehow as a member. Accordingly, the management could not be in the hands of private individuals, as parliamentarism presupposes. It was an office and the politician in charge was a civil servant, a servant of the whole. In England, politics and business interest coincided; in France, the swarm of professional politicians that soon appeared with the constitution was recruited by the interest groups. In Prussia, the pure professional politician has always been a disreputable phenomenon. If, therefore, with the 19th century a democratisation of the state became indispensable, it could not take place in English forms, which corresponded to the very opposite system. Democracy here could not mean private freedom, which coincided with business freedom and necessarily had to lead to private politics, for which the state served as a tool. If the idea of the order 'all for all' was given a modern version, it was not the formation of parties which, by way of elections every few years, gave the people the right to vote once for the candidate appointed by the party or not at all, while upwards they intervened as opposition in the work of government, but it was the principle of assigning to each individual, according to his practical, moral, intellectual abilities, a certain measure of command and obedience, a quite personal degree and rank of responsibility, therefore, which was revocable at any time, like an office. This is the 'council system' as planned a hundred years ago by Baron von Stein[54], a genuine Prussian idea based on the principles of selection, co-responsibility, collegiality. Today it has been dragged, quite Marxistically, into the mire of class egoism, a mere reversal of the picture Marx had drawn of the robber class of English-style capitalists, of Vikings without state control, a free trade system from below with the working class as society and thus English through and through. This is Bentham, not Kant.

Stein and his Kant-trained advisers were thinking of an organisation of the professions. In a country where work was to be the general duty and content of life, people distinguished themselves according to their performance, not their possessions. So local professional bodies according to the importance of these professions in the nation as a whole; higher representations up to a supreme council of state; mandates revocable at any time; so no organised parties, no professional politicians, no periodic elections. Stein did not express these ideas; he would perhaps have denied them in this version, but they lay as a germ in the reforms which he proposed, and they would have been suitable for carrying out a planned democratisation of the Prussian system, such as corresponded to its own instincts, not those of England and France, and such as would have guaranteed a selection of the personalities gifted precisely for this system. To a state belongs a council of state. It is the relation of the machine to the learned engineer. To a non-state belongs the secret council of individual parties constituted in exactly the same way, each of which must at all times be able to make its apparatus work as the government of the country. England, indeed, has *two* 'Labour Councils' or Crown Councils instead of one,

---

54 Heinrich Friedrich Karl vom und zum Stein (1757–1831) was a Prussian civil servant who, as a senior minister of state, initiated numerous reforms in Prussia that have shaped the German state to this day. — *Transl.*

and that is the meaning of parliamentarism[55]. The Prussian system would have required one of stable composition.

Instead of this, under the impression of the Napoleonic events, the admiration of English institutions has now become dominant. Hardenberg[56], Humboldt and the others were 'English'. Instead of Kant, Shaftesbury and Hume[57] came to the fore. Where a reorganisation would have been necessary and possible from within, it was carried out from without. All the political bitterness of the 19th century, the boundless barrenness of our parliamentarism in men, thoughts and achievements, the constant struggle between fundamentally hostile opposition and forcible imposition stem from the fact that a strict and humanly profound order was imposed on a people who were gifted for a quite different, equally strict and profound order. Wherever the old Prussian creative power was able to test itself *freely* on great matters, as in the organisation of the syndicates and cartels, the trade unions, in social policy, it showed what it was capable of achieving.

How alien parliamentarism has remained to the Prussian and, since 1870, to the German people, is shown by the indifference with which, despite all the efforts of the press and parties, the elections and the questions of suffrage have been received. It was very often only the expression of vague annoyance when people made use of their right to vote, and in no other country do these English-style election days give such a false picture of the real attitude. The people have never become accustomed to this way of 'cooperating' which is foreign to them, and never will. If an Englishman does not follow the proceedings of

---

55 The voters have not the slightest influence on the composition of the two councils. They only decide which of them should govern.

56 Karl August von Hardenberg (1750–1822) was a Prussian statesman and reformer. — *Transl.*

57 David Hume (1711–1776) was a Scottish philosopher, economist and historian. He was one of the most important representatives of the Scottish Enlightenment. His sceptical and metaphysics-free philosophy inspired Immanuel Kant to write his *Critique of Pure Reason.* — *Transl.*

Parliament, he does so in the knowledge that his interests are well served there. When a German does so, he does so with a feeling of complete indifference. For him, only 'the government' is something essential. Parliamentarism will always remain a system of externals with us.

In England, the two parties had been absolute leaders of politics. Here, however, there was a *state*, and the parties, which were now founded for the sake of the parliamentary method, whereas in England the method had developed out of the actual constitution of the trading people, were merely *critical* of it. From the outset there was a disproportion between the system which was to be introduced and that which existed, between the intention and the effect of the method, between the concept and the essence of the parties. The English opposition is a necessary part of the government; it works in a complementary way. Our opposition is *real* negation not only of the opposing parties but of the government itself. This has not changed at all with the abolition of the monarchy.

It is significant and betrays the strength of the national instinct that the two parties which may be called specifically Prussian, the conservative and the socialist, have never lost an illiberal and anti-parliamentary tendency. They are *both* socialist in a higher sense, and thus quite corresponding to *both* capitalist parties of England. They do not recognise private and party management of the government, but assign to the *whole* the unconditional authority to regulate the conduct of life of the individual in the general interest. The fact that some speak of the monarchical state, others of the working people, is a difference in words in view of the fact that here *everyone* works and that the individual will is *always* subject to the will of the whole. These two parties, under the pressure of the English system, were states within the state; they were, according to their conviction, *the* state, and therefore did not recognise at all the right of parties other than their own to exist. This in itself precluded parliamentary government. They did not deny the soldierly spirit; they organised united, well-disciplined battalions of voters, in which the conservatives were better officers, the socialists better men. They were built on command and obedience and conceived of *their* state, the Hohenzollern state and the future state in the same way. Freedom was no more 'English' freedom in the one than in the other. A deep contempt for the English parliamentary nature, for the hierarchy of wealth and poverty, pervades their nothing less than parliamentary effectiveness. They both despised Prussian suffrage with its bitter gradation of rich and poor — the Conservatives thinking it just good enough as a means — but they basically despised any English-style electoral system because they knew it would inevitably lead to a plutocracy. Those who can pay for such systems reap their fruits.

Alongside them was the Spanish-style party, the papal one, whose intellectual tradition goes back to the times of Habsburg world domination and the territorial spirit of the Peace of Westphalia. In Napoleon it secretly worshipped the founder of the Confederation of the Rhine. In its tactics, a remnant of the masterly cabinet diplomacy of Madrid and Vienna is still alive; it has understood how to make democratic tendencies and parliamentary customs *serviceable* to itself with the mature cleverness of the Counter-Reformation. It despises nothing; it knows how to find a successful side to everything. And let us not forget the socialist discipline of the Spanish spirit, which, like the Prussian, emerged from the knightly orders of the Gothic period and before it had summed up a world thought in the formula 'throne and altar'.

And finally the intellectual Englishness of Germany constituted itself as a party in order to champion genuine parliamentarism with the fervour of a world-view, as a principle, as an idea, as a thing in itself. Napoleon was to them the bringer of liberal ideas. They exercised their 'point of view' wherever the Englishman would have exercised his talents and experience. The 'point of view' is their symbol. When three liberals get together, they form a new party. That is *their* concept of individualism. They do not join a bowling club without 'putting on the agenda' a change in the statutes. Because in England there is a stateless order of public things, any act of authority by the state is sure to provoke their indignation. Even in socialism they still hate authoritative ends. This bourgeoisie is a specifically German phenomenon. It should not have been confused with the French bourgeoisie and still less with the English middle class. The grand style of English liberalism suits it badly. *Quod licet Iovi, non licet bovi*[58]. Under the frock coat of the free-minded man there is still alive something of the soul of old imperial cities, which raises a constant painful protest against the realities of modern civilisation, and which heaps around it an immense literature in which something transcendent and ideal — something different in every book — is interpreted into the English ideas, which are hard as reality, without which one could not resist the equally unromantic hardness of Prussian ideas. And this politically harmless sense of freedom, incapable of any organisation, that other liberalism, which borrowed from the wholeness of English nature only the purely economic dictatorship of private wealth, without its moral content as an aim, now really combined into a fighting party, which it set up for a slowly eroding, wearying, murdering opposition wherever the socialist thought of the Prussian state stood in the way of the sovereignty of business. It was its spirit, in the end, that rallied the 'inner England' of the majority parties to that parliamentary revolution of 1917, which secured the final victory for the outer England of the Entente powers by overthrowing the state. It demands pure parliamentarism, not because it wants a free state, but because it wants no state, and because it knows as well as England that a socialistically inclined people becomes incapable of action with this foreign skirt on its body. The 'supranational' cosmopolitanism of the German Michel suits it perfectly. Even if it laughs at it as an end, it appreciates it as a means. It hands over the cathedra and the feuilleton to the cosmopolitan professor, and politics 'above the line' and in the boardroom to the parliamentary dilettante.

---

58   Latin: 'What is permitted to Jupiter is not permitted to the oxen.' — *Transl.*

With this two-man team it drives towards the goal of consummate Englishness. Socialism has suffered its heaviest defeat in the German Revolution; the enemy has brought it to turn its weapon against itself.

In spite of all this, the two great world thoughts continue to oppose each other: dictatorship of money or of organisation, the world as booty or as state, wealth or authority, success or profession. The *two* socialist parties of Germany must come together against the enemy of the common idea, against the inner England: capitalist-parliamentary liberalism. A socialist monarchy[59] — for authoritative socialism is monarchical; the most responsible place in the immense organism, the place of the *first servant of this state* according to the words of Frederick the Great, must not be handed over to private striving — a unity, in which each according to his *socialist* rank, his talent for voluntary discipline from inner superiority, his organisational ability, his labour power, conscientiousness and energy, his intelligent common feeling, receives the place which is due to him; the general duty to work, and thereupon an occupational division, which is at the same time administration and has a supreme administrative council instead of parliament — where all work, officers, civil servants, peasants, miners, may it be called a workers' council — this is an idea which has slowly matured in the Faustian world of man and has long since bred its type of man.

On the other side is the capitalist world republic — for England *is* a republic; republic *today* means government by the successful private man who can pay for his election and thus his influence — and the surface of the earth as the hunting ground of those who want to become rich and demand for themselves the possibility of free individual struggle. And there Tories and Whigs, the *two* capitalist parties, will at last unite against the 'inner Prussia' of socialism, which over there does not even have the working classes all to itself — and remember

---

59 It was Lassalle who, in 1862, demanded the union of Prussian royalty with the workers to fight against liberalism and the English 'night watchman theory' of the weak state.

that labour is a misfortune there. This means a rearrangement of the parliamentary system, which cannot work with three parties. In Old England it was rich against rich, one world-view against the other *within* the upper class. Now it is rich against poor, England — against something else. But with this the form of parliamentarism is *used up*; there is no doubt possible. It was already in decline in England when German folly brought it over. It had its best period before Bismarck. It was an old, mature, genteel, infinitely refined form, which required all the tact of the English gentleman of good breeding to be mastered to perfection. The condition was a self-evident agreement on so many questions that differences did not endanger civility. The parliamentary struggle had something of the good forms of a duel among aristocrats about it. It is like the old music from Bach to Beethoven: it was based on a perfect musical culture down to the fingertips. As soon as the rigour of this culture waned, the music became barbaric. Today, no one can write an old-style fugue with the old ease and self-evidence of mastering all the rules in one go. And so it is with the fugal style of parliamentary tactics. Coarser people, coarser questions — and all is over. The duel turns into a brawl. With the people of old breeding, the institutions, the *felt* forms, the tact also come to an end. The new parliamentarism will present the struggle for existence in very little restrained forms and with much worse success. The relationship of the party leaders to the party, of the party to the masses, will be cruder, more transparent, more unvarnished. *This is the beginning of caesarism.* It is already foreshadowed in the English elections of 1918. We shall not escape it any more. It is our fate as well as the Roman, the Chinese, that of all mature civilisations. But billionaires or generals, bankers or officials of the greatest stature — that is the eternal question.

MARX

18

This mighty final struggle of the two Germanic ideas is now thwarted by a completely different factor: the workers' question. There it is a most inner opposition of world-views that urges a decision in order to impose a final unified form on the being of Faustian man; here it is a material emergency that demands a change in the external conditions of life. In a sense, the one is metaphysics, the other national economy. The *difference in rank* of the two phenomena is thus established.

The problem of the 'fourth estate' appears in every culture at its transition to civilisation. For us it begins with the 19ᵗʰ century; Rousseau is suddenly obsolete. The third estate belongs to the city, which places itself on an equal footing with the countryside, the fourth to the cosmopolitan city, which destroys the countryside. It is the spiritually uprooted people of very late conditions, which surges nomadically through these stony labyrinths as a formless and hostile mass, sucking up the remnants of living humanity all around it, homeless, bitter and miserable, full of hatred for the strong gradations of old culture to which it has become numb, longing for liberation from its impossible existence.

The civilisation of Western Europe is dominated by machine industry in all the expressions and forms of its entire existence. The industrial worker is by no means the 'fourth estate', but he rightly feels himself to be the representative of this estate. He is a symbol. He has arisen as a type with this civilisation and he feels the deplorable state of his existence most deeply. If others are slaves of the technical age, the engineer as well as the entrepreneur, he is *the* slave.

But there is no solution of the labour question for the worker alone and through him alone. The fourth estate in itself is a mere fact, not an idea. In the face of a fact, there are only material compromises, not as the effect and realisation of any ideals, but as the strategic results of a long struggle for advantage at the expense of others, which finally leads to a kind of standstill, in which one resignedly accepts the situation as it has finally arisen after all the contingencies of the struggle, in order to find in it a small happiness of habituation, a Chinese happiness, the happiness of Roman imperial times: *panem et circenses.* Today this is difficult to understand, because we are at the height of metropolitan mass excitement, and the close observer, as a result of the noise of the catchwords, overestimates the *one-sided prospects of class egoism*, but in a century or two it will all be over unless the workers' movement enters into the service of a general idea. What was left of the passions of the Gracian period under Augustus? The problem had not been solved; it had disintegrated.

This is now where Marx comes in. He has attempted by a brilliant construction, more startling than correct, to raise the fact to the status of an idea. Over the mighty antithesis of Vikingism and the spirit of the Order he spans a thin but firmly established theory and thus creates a popular picture of history, which, in fact, dominates the views of the present to a large extent. He came from the Prussian atmosphere and settled in the English one, but he has remained equally alien to the soul of both peoples. As a man of the scientific 19th century, he was a good materialist and a bad psychologist. And so, in the end, he did not fill the great realities with the content of an idea, but reduced the ideas to concepts, to interests. Instead of English blood, which he did not feel in himself, he saw only English things and concepts, and of Hegel, who represented a good piece of Prussian state thinking, only the method had been accessible to him. And so, by a truly grotesque combination, he transferred the *instinctive antagonism of the two Germanic races to the material antagonism of two classes. He attributed the Prussian idea of socialism to the 'proletariat', the fourth class, and the English idea of capitalism to the 'bourgeoisie', the third class.* It was only from this system that the fixed meaning of the four terms emerged, as is familiar to everyone today. Through these catchwords, irresistible in their simplicity, he has succeeded in consolidating the working class of almost all countries into a class with a pronounced class consciousness. In his language speaks, in his terms thinks today the fourth estate. Proletariat was no longer a name, but a task. The future was henceforth viewed through a piece of literature. In the superficiality of the system lies its strength. Although there is still a Spanish ecclesiastical, an English capitalist and a Prussian authoritarian socialism, and proletarian movements of an anarchic, capitalist and genuine socialist character, one does not know it. Belief in the unity of purpose is stronger than reality and, as always in the West, it clings to a book whose absolute truth is a crime to doubt. Only the printed word guarantees the effect of the Faustian spirit in all distances of space and time. In the English Revolution it was the Bible, in the French one Rousseau's *Contrat social*, in the German one *The Communist Manifesto*. From the reinterpretation of the opposition of races into that of classes and of old Germanic instincts into the very recent needs of metropolitan populations, the decisive *concept of class struggle* now arises. The horizontal direction of historical forces becomes vertical: this is the meaning of the materialist conception of history. The natural-scientific thinking of this time demands the opposition of force and substance: the substances of political forces are called peoples, the substances of economic forces are called classes. Marxism exchanges the rank of the two forces and thus also the rank of the two substances. In this way, however, the word class acquires a completely new meaning.

With all the psychological incomprehension of a scientifically trained head of 1850, Marx knows nothing about the difference between rank and class. A rank is an ethical concept, the expression of an *idea*. The privileged of 1789 stood opposite the bourgeoisie as a *class* that embodied an ideal of form, *grandeur*, *courtoisie*[60], inner and outer nobility, no matter what decay had left of it. The bourgeoisie denied the *ethical* superiority of the old noble manners, and only from

---

60   French: 'courtesy'. — *Transl.*

this did the rejection of social privilege follow. The English-trained mind of the Parisians opposed it with another ideal, and French instinct created from it the principle of equality in the *ethical* sense. This was the new meaning of the term 'human society', namely equality and the general binding force of the *moral* ideal, which was based on reason and nature and not on blood and tradition.

Class, however, is a purely economic concept, and from it the *ethical-political* concept of the bourgeoisie of 1789 is reversed into the *economic* one of 1850. The ideal of class has become class interest. Only in England had the classes long been graded according to wealth. The middle class comprised those who lived from their labour without being poor. The upper class was rich without working. The lower class worked and was poor. In Prussia, however, it was *position*, a greater or lesser degree of command and obedience, that divided the classes. Here, in addition to the peasantry, there was a civil servant class, i.e. not an economic class at all, but a unity of function. The essence of modern France, on the other hand, is the *non-existence of real classes*. The nation is a disordered mass from which rich and poor stand out, but without forming a class. The whole nation is a class, not of the strictness of Germanic stratifications, but still a single one.

Marx thus thinks in purely English terms. His two-class system is drawn from the situation of a merchant people who sacrificed their agriculture to trade and who never had a state civil service with a pronounced — Prussian — consciousness of class. Here there are only 'bourgeois' and 'proletarians', *subjects and objects of business*, robbers and robbed, quite Viking-like. Applied to the realm of Prussian state thought, these terms are nonsense. Marx would not have been able to distinguish the idea, following from the principle of 'all for all', that each individual, without distinction of position, is a servant of the whole, of the state, from the fact of English industrial slavery. He took the *mere external image* of Prussianism: organisation, discipline, commonality, something quite independent of an individual class, a technical form, socialism, in order to hand it over as the aim and weapon of labour in an English-ordered society, so that it might, again quite Viking-like, exchange the roles of robbers and robbed — expropriation of the expropriators — with a very egoistic programme of division of the spoils after victory to boot.

Awkwardness is still the precise definition of the two classes. Bourgeoisie means something quite different within the Marxist circle of thought than in that of Rousseau. There is a great difference between using it in opposition to the privileged of the feudal period and from the standpoint of the urban working masses. In terms of the three estates of 1789, there is no longer a fourth; in terms of the fourth of today, there is no longer a first and a second. Sieyès[61] had calculated the clergy at 80,000, the nobility at 120,000, the third estate at 25 million heads. According to this, the last was *the* people. Bourgeoisie means 'all'. The French peasant is also a bourgeois.

The fourth estate, however, is a minority and cannot even be sharply separated, for depending on the designation — manual worker, industrial worker, proletarian, mass — the boundaries are different. It is sometimes defined and even more often perceived as being quite different from the bourgeoisie — it is again 'all' with the exception of the entrepreneurs.

The third estate was actually a negation. It wants to say that there should no longer be any estates. The fourth estate, however, abolishes this equality. It places a single occupational class as authoritative in social life; it reaches back beyond 1789 and presents itself again as a privileged class. This lies in the concept of the dictatorship of the proletariat: rule by a class that is by no means certain of its numerical superiority. Thus the class goal is transformed back into a caricature of the old class ideal. It is only literature, not blood and education, which speaks from these constructions, but the ridiculousness of the German Revolution, the workers' councils as a new House of Lords,

---

61   Emmanuel Joseph Sieyès (1748–1836) was a French priest, statesman, and one of the main theorists of the French Revolution. His best-known work was *Qu'est-ce que le Tiers État?* (What is the Third Estate?). — *Transl.*

the elevation of the worker to the status of English gentleman through the strike with continuous payment of wages have shown, as in the time of Cromwell and Robespierre, that literature can temporarily become grotesque reality.

19

But Marx's morality is also of English origin. Marxism betrays in every sentence that it comes from a theological and not a political way of thinking. His economic theory is only the consequence of a basic ethical feeling, and the materialist conception of history forms only the final chapter of a philosophy whose roots reach back to the English Revolution with its biblical mood, which has remained binding on English thought ever since.

Thus it is that its basic concepts are felt to be moral opposites. The words *socialism* and *capitalism* denote the good and evil of this irreligious religion. The bourgeois is the devil, the wage-worker the angel of a new mythology, and one need only delve a little into the vulgar pathos of *The Communist Manifesto* to recognise Independent Christianity behind the mask. Social evolution is the 'will of God'. The 'final goal' used to be called eternal bliss, the 'collapse of bourgeois society' the Last Judgement.

Thus Marx teaches *contempt for labour*. Perhaps he did not even feel this. Work, hard, long, tedious work is a misfortune, effortless acquisition is happiness. Behind the genuinely English disdain for the man who has only his hands to live by is the instinct of the Viking, whose occupation is to make booty, not to mend his sails. Therefore in England the manual labourer is more of a slave than anywhere else. He is so *morally*; he feels that his acquisition excludes him from the name of gentleman. In the terms *bourgeoisie* and *proletariat* the purely English valuations of *merchant profit and manual labour*[62] are opposed

---

62   And not of manual labour and mental labour. As with Tories and Whigs, the 'mental worker' also has to take a stand on these economic parties, and in England of the time he opted — as a gentleman — for mercantilism.

to each other. The one is happiness, the other unhappiness, the one genteel, the other mean. But the hatred of the unfortunate says: the first is the profession of evil, the second of good.

And this explains Marx's state of mind, from which his critique of society emerged and which made him so fatal to genuine socialism. He knew the essence of labour only in English terms, as the means of getting rich, as a means without moral depth, for only success, money, the grace of God made visible, was of ethical significance. The Englishman lacks the sense of the dignity of rigorous work. It degrades, it is an ugly necessity — woe to him who has nothing but it, who possesses nothing without ever new labour, and above all, who *will* never possess anything. If Marx had understood the meaning of Prussian labour, of activity for its own sake, as service in the name of the whole, for 'all' and not for oneself, as a duty that ennobles regardless of the *kind* of work, his *Manifesto* would probably never have been written.

But here he was supported by his Jewish instinct, which he himself marked in his writing on the Jewish question. *The curse of physical labour* at the beginning of Genesis, the prohibition against *desecrating* Sunday by work, this made the Old Testament pathos of narrow feeling accessible to him. And hence his hatred of those who do not need to work. The socialism of Fichte would despise them as idlers, as superfluous, forgetful of duty, parasites of life, but the instinct of Marx *envies* them. They have it too good and that is why one should revolt against them. He has inculcated in the proletariat a disregard for labour. His most fanatical disciples want the destruction of the whole culture in order to reduce the quantity of indispensable labour as much as possible. Luther praised the simplest labour activity as pleasing to God, Goethe the 'demand of the day'; but before the eyes of Marx hovers the ideal of the Epicurean proletarian who possesses everything effortlessly — this is the ultimate meaning of that expropriation of the blissful. And he is right about the English instinct. What the English call happiness, business success, which saves physical labour, which thus makes a man a gentleman, should go to all — Englishmen. For us this is vile, the taste of mob and snob.

This ethic dominates his economic ideas. His thinking is thoroughly Manchesterian; it is perfectly like Cobden's, who was just then leading the Whigs' free trade doctrine to victory. Marx combats capitalism, which takes its justification from Bentham and Shaftesbury and has it formulated by Adam Smith; but since he is only a critic, negating and uncreative, he receives his principle from the very thing he negates.

Labour is a commodity to him, not a 'duty': that is the core of his national economy. His morality becomes business morality. It is not that business is immoral, but that the worker was a fool not to do it, one reads between the lines. And the worker has understood. The wage struggle becomes speculation, the worker becomes a trader in his commodity 'labour'. The secret of the famous phrase of surplus value is that it is perceived as *booty* which the trader of the other party carries off. One does not begrudge it to him. Class egoism is elevated to a principle. The manual worker not only wants to trade, but he *wants to dominate the market*. The genuine Marxist is hostile to the state for exactly the same reason as the Whig: it hinders him in the ruthless championing of his private business interests. Marxism is the capitalism of labour. Think of Darwin, who is as close intellectually to Marx as Malthus and Cobden. Trade is always conceived as a struggle for existence. In industry, the entrepreneur trades in the commodity 'money', the manual worker in the commodity 'labour'. Marx wants to deprive capital of the right to private interests, but he only knows how to replace it with the workers' right to private interests. This is unsocialist, but genuinely English.

For Marx has become English in this too: *the state does not appear in his thinking*. He thinks in terms of society, without the state. As in the political-parliamentary existence of England, so in the economic life of his world there is only a system of two sovereign parties, nothing that stands *above* the parties. So there is only struggle, no arbitration, only victory or defeat, only the dictatorship of one of the two parties conceivable. The *Manifesto* wants to replace the dictatorship of the capitalist, the evil party, with that of the proletarian, the good. Marx does not see the possibility of others.

But the Prussian socialist state stands beyond this good and evil. It is the *whole* people, and to its unconditional sovereignty both parties are only — parties, minorities, *both* serving the general public. Socialism is, in purely technical terms, the civil service principle. Every worker ultimately acquires the character of a civil servant instead of a merchant, every entrepreneur likewise. There are industrial officials and commercial officials as well as military and transport officials. This has been carried out on the largest scale in Egyptian culture and again quite differently in Chinese culture. It is the *inner* form of the political civilisation of the West and already symbolically expressed in the Gothic cities with their fraternities and guilds, already in the system of Gothic cathedrals, where every small link is a necessary part of a dynamic whole. Marx did not understand this. His horizon and his intellectual creative power only reached so far as to turn a private merchant *society* into a private worker *society*. As a critic of the first rank, he is impotent as a creator. His constant evasion of the question of how he imagines the form of government of this gigantic world mechanism, his amateurish praise of the 'council system' of the Paris Commune of 1871, which arose from the special conditions of a besieged city and was not viable, prove it. The creative is not learned. You either have it or you do not. The entire social democracy of the 19th century produced only *one* creator of great style, *one* politician who knew not how to write but how to govern: Bebel, certainly not the most intelligent of his party, but its first and only organiser. For a ruler, quite different talents come into consideration than intelligence in the literary sense. Napoleon did not tolerate 'book writers' around him.

From the economic Darwinism of the Englishman and the two-class system of Marx now arises the natural weapon in the struggle between mercantilism and the trading labour force: *the strike*. Through the strike, the commodity 'labour' is denied to the buyer. Through the strike of the other party, the lockout, the commodity 'money' is denied to the buyer. A reserve army of workers assures the buyers of money, a reserve army of entrepreneurs (labour shortage) assures the buyers of labour their sales. The strike is the *unsocialist* characteristic of Marxism, the classical characteristic of its origin in a merchant philosophy to which Marx belonged out of instinct and habituation.

In the *state*, on the other hand, labour is not a commodity but a duty to the community, and there is — this is *Prussian* democratisation — no difference in the moral dignity of labour: the judge and scholar 'work' as well as the miner and iron turner. It was therefore English thought that in the German Revolution the manual labourer exploited the rest of the people by extorting as much money as possible for as little work as possible and wanted to raise his 'commodity' in importance above any other. In the means of struggle of the strike lies the presupposition that there is no people as a state, but only parties. Marxist, i.e. English, is the idea of free wage struggle and, after the victory of the proletarian party, the unilateral sovereign fixing of wages.

The *Prussian* idea is the *impartial state fixing of wages for every kind of work*, graded according to the overall economic situation, in the interest of the people as a whole and not of a single occupational class. This is the principle of the civil servants' salary scale, applied to all workers. It includes the *prohibition of the strike* as an anti-state and mercantile private means. The fixing of wages must be taken away from employers and workers and entrusted to a general economic council, so that both can count on a fixed figure, as has long been the case with other variables of management and the standard of living[63].

---

63 A system could be envisaged whereby every working person, the officer and administrative official as well as the 'manual worker', would have an account at a kind of state and savings bank, to which the uniform amounts are to be transferred in their entirety by those obliged to pay. The individual is then

Marxism is senseless in the face of the *innate* forms of Prussian socialist man. It can deny and weaken them, but they will finally prove stronger than the theoretical, like everything living and natural. In the realm of English being, however, it is at home; here it is better understood than genuine socialism, and here, with the *serious* opening of the duel of economic parties, old-style parliamentarism is at an end. The two parties of wealth, formed by the upper class, were *politically* constituted and in the last analysis united on economic questions. Even the struggle over the free trade system, in which the Whigs were victorious around 1850, the last period of classical parliamentarism, was fought out in consummate forms. Tories and Whigs differed only in preferring war and submission or commercial penetration, the courage or cunning of the pirate. But now an economic antagonism forms two new parties — of money and of labour — and this struggle can *no longer* be waged by parliamentary means. Here it is no longer the form but the cause that is in dispute, and if one does not want to submit to an alien principle, that of the state as a non-party authority, there is only the final suppression of one economic party by the other.

20

Marx has now extended the already highly schematic picture of industrial England, taken from a very questionable point of view, over the whole of history. He asserts the validity of his economic constructions for the *whole* of 'human society', adding that they are the only essential thing in the course of history. In this he resembles Darwin, who also started from Malthus and claimed his system to be valid for 'all organisms', when in fact it only fits the more human-like higher animals and becomes absurd when details such as breeding selection, mimicry and heredity are seriously applied to fission fungi and coral animals.

---

credited with an amount graded according to seniority and the number of family members.

The materialistic conception of history, which takes the economic situation as the cause (in the physical meaning of the word), and religion, law, custom, art, science as the effects, undoubtedly has something convincing in this late stage, because it addresses the thinking of irreligious and traditionless metropolitan people: not that the economic situation is really the 'cause', but that art and religion have become powerless, empty, external, and now in fact act as shadows of the only vigorously developed form of expression of the time. But this is precisely what *is* English: religion as 'cant', art as 'comfort' for the upper class and as alms for the lower class ('art for the people') have penetrated into the other countries with the English way of life.

But Hegel is above, his disciple Marx below the level of historical factuality. If one eliminates Hegel's metaphysics, there appears a thinker on the state with such a strong sense of reality as there is no other in modern philosophy. As a 'Prussian' out of an intellectual affinity of choice, he places the state at the centre of his very profound, almost Goethean development with the same certainty as Marx, as an electoral Englishman, places the economy at the centre of his mechanical-Darwinian 'evolution' (in German: 'Fortschritt[64]'). *With Hegel, the state is the history maker; politics is history.* 'Human society' is not his word. The high officials of Bismarck's generation were for the most part strict Hegelians. Marx, however, thinks of *history without the state*, history as the arena of parties, history as the conflict of economic private interests. Materialist conception of history is English conception of history, the aspect of an unbound Viking and merchant people.

But the intellectual premises of this way of thinking are no longer present today. The 19th century was that of natural science; the 20th belongs to psychology. We no longer believe in the power of reason over life. We feel that life dominates reason. Knowledge of human nature is more important to us than abstract and general ideals; optimists have

---

64 'Progress'. — *Transl.*

become sceptics: it is not what should come, but what will come that concerns us; and remaining masters of the facts is more important to us than becoming slaves to ideals. The logic of the image of nature, the concatenation of cause and effect, seems superficial to us; only the logic of the organic, fate, the instinct that one feels, whose omnipotence one beholds in the change of things, testifies to the depth of becoming. Marxism is an ideology. It also bears the signs of it in its division of history, which the materialist retained from Christianity after the power of faith had been extinguished. From antiquity through the Middle Ages to modern times leads the path of evolution, at the end of which stands realised Marxism, the earthly paradise. It is worthless to refute this picture. What matters is to give modern man a *new* view, from which necessarily a new image follows of its own accord. Life has no 'goal'. Humanity has no 'goal'. The existence of the world, in which we spin off a small episode on our little planet, is something far too sublime for paltriness such as 'the happiness of most' to be the goal and purpose. The greatness of the play lies in its purposelessness. That is how Goethe felt about it. But to fulfil this life that is given to us, this reality around us in which we are placed by fate, with the highest possible content, to live in such a way that we may be proud of ourselves, to act in such a way that something of us lives on in this consummating reality, that is the task. We are not 'human beings in themselves'. That belongs to the past ideology. Cosmopolitanism is a miserable word. We are people of one century, one nation, one circle, one type. These are the necessary conditions under which we can give meaning and depth to existence, be doers, even through the word *doers*. The more we fill these *given* limits, the wider is our effect. Plato was Athenian, Caesar was Roman, Goethe was German: the fact that they were *wholly and first of all* so was the precondition of their world-historical effect.

From this standpoint, in the midst of the German Revolution, we today contrast Marxism and socialism. Socialism, the still misunderstood Prussianism, is a piece of reality of the highest order; Marx is literature. A literature becomes obsolete; a reality triumphs or dies. Compare the socialist criticism at the international congresses with a socialist fact, the Bebel Party. The saying that ideas make world history is, as it should be understood, interested literary talk. Ideas are not spoken. The artist looks, the thinker feels, the statesman and soldier realise them. Ideas become conscious only through the blood, libidinously, not through abstract reflection. They testify to their existence through the style of peoples, the type of people, the symbolism of deeds and works, and whether these people know about them at all, whether they speak and write about them or not, rightly or wrongly, that matters little. *Life* is first and last, and life has no system, no programme, no reason; it is there for itself and through itself, and the deep order in which it realises itself can only be looked at and felt — and then perhaps described, but not dissected according to good and evil, right or wrong, useful and desirable.

That is why Marxism is not an idea. In it, visible signs and forms of two ideas are put together intellectually and therefore arbitrarily. This *way of thinking* is temporary. It has been effective because every people has used these concepts as a weapon. Again, it does not matter whether they were understood or not. They were effective because the sound of the words and the force of the sentences made people believe in something. In what — that was again the unchanging idea of one's own life, one's own blood.

Marxism collapses today with the resounding orgy of its attempt at reality. *The Communist Manifesto*, with the year 1918, has become just as much a literary curiosity as the *Contrat social* with the year 1793. Real, instinctive socialism as an expression of old Prussian nature, which literarily strayed to England and dried up into an anti-English theory, is today returning to the consciousness of its origin and its meaning.

'THE INTERNATIONAL'

21

Later on, even that which today dominates the political image of the world as international socialism will be viewed with irony. What is really there — the *International of slogans, Marxism as a phrase* — is only able to awaken a sense of togetherness in the workers of all countries for decades, and even then only to a much lesser degree than the noise of the congresses and the confidence of the appeals would suggest. In reality, unity is limited to the belief that it exists and to the fact that a movement in one country often gives rise to such movements in others, where the same thing is supposedly striven for. But it is characteristic of a civilisation as saturated with literature as the present one that mass leaders who live in a constant fog of theories can nevertheless become bearers of very strong realities. At these congresses of lies, the representatives of English, French, German, Russian attitudes to life come together again and again, without somehow understanding each other in the ultimate reasons of wanting and feeling, to agree on a certain stock of propositions under which they believe they mean and demand the same thing.

How thinly this intellectual reality is spread over the other of the national instincts was shown in August 1914, when it evaporated in *one* day under the sudden heat of natural and not spiritual passions. Socialism is something different in every country. There are as many working-class movements as there are today living races in the spiritual sense, and they reject each other with the same hatred as the peoples themselves, as soon as it is a question of more than the establishment of common hatred. There are red Jacobins and red Puritans, a red Versailles, a red Potsdam. There is the same distance between Shaw and Bebel as between Rhodes and Bismarck. It is always only the same theoretical fabric from which they all make their clothes.

In the World War it was not only the Entente that was directed against Germany, but also the *pseudo-socialism of the Entente countries*, which was directed against the real one, the Prussian one, in Germany. *In the person of the Kaiser, real socialism betrayed itself, its origin, its meaning, its position in the socialist world.* Bebel would have felt this and prevented it. His epigones did not understand. Today they go to the congresses of lies and sign the Treaty of Versailles once more in the realm of the phrase. Prussian-German socialism has its most dangerous opponent *not* in German capitalism — which had strong socialist features in it and which *it has itself* pushed into English forms only since 1917, most strongly perhaps by the loosening of the masterly organised trade unions and the introduction of local works councils, behind the concession of which the majority socialists seek to hide their liberal-parliamentary tendency from the masses — but in what is being pushed in the home of capitalism under the name of socialism. What Engels saw with his sharp eyes, that there is *only* German socialism, the present-day spokesmen of German socialism have forgotten, and they seek to prove it by Michel-like servility to the Entente socialists.

In fact, the French socialism of coups and sabotages is a mere feeling of social revenge, which has already found its Clémenceaus in the Paris Commune uprising, the English one a reform capitalism, the German one only a world-view. The Frenchman remains an anarchist, the Englishman liberal, and above all the French and English worker is *first* French and English, and only then, perhaps, theoretically, a supporter of the International. The *born* socialist, the Prussian worker[65], has always been the fool of others. He alone took the phrase seriously as only some professor took the phrases of the Church of St. Paul. He *alone* — who could point to a grandiose creation: his party — was the devout listener of the others and helped pay for their strikes.

---

65 There is a deep meaning in Bebel's words when he once called Munich the Capua of German Social Democracy. He would have found confirmation in the carnival of the council period.

A *true* International is only possible through the victory of the idea of *one* race over all others, and not through the dissolution of all opinions into a colourless mass. Let us at last be sceptics and throw away the old ideology. There are no reconciliations in real history. Those who believe in them must feel an eternal horror of the fool's dance of events, and they only take refuge in self-deception if they think they can ever conjure it up by treaties. There is only *one* end to the eternal struggle: death. The death of the individual, the death of a nation, the death of a culture. Ours lies far ahead of us in the uncertain darkness of the next millennium. We Germans, who are placed in this century, interwoven in our existence with that of Faustian civilisation, have rich, untapped possibilities in us and enormous tasks before us. Together with the International, which is *irrevocably* preparing itself, we have the idea of world organisation, of the world state, the English that of world trusteeship and world exploitation, the French nothing to give. We stand up for this not with our speeches, but with our *existence*. The Order idea of *genuine* socialism stands and falls with Prussianism. Only the Church still carries the old Spanish universal idea, the protection and care of all peoples in the shadow of Catholicism. From the days of the Hohenstaufen era looms the image of a gigantic struggle between a political and a religious world thought. At this moment, however, the third, Viking thought is triumphing in the British lion: the world not as a state, not as a church, but as prey.

The real International is imperialism, domination of Faustian civilisation, that is, of the *whole* earth, by a single formative principle, not by equalisation and concession, but by victory and annihilation. Socialism has capitalism and papalism beside and against it, three *kinds* of socialist will to power: through the state, money, the Church. They have their forces in the political, economic and religious consciousnesses, each of which seeks to classify the other two: these are the creative instincts of Prussian, English and Spanish man, and they reach back from the spiritual coldness and height of modern civilisation to those early libidinous men of Gothic times who subdued the Markish marshes with sword and plough, cruised the northern sea in their frail barges, and waged the war of faith against the Moors south of the Pyrenees. Markish, English and Spanish Gothic styles bear witness to a different soul from that of the French. These instincts are more powerful than anything else and can even outlive the peoples in which they have created visible symbols. There was a Roman spirit even at a time when real Romans no longer existed. The Spanish spirit as a people is powerless, but as a Church it stands in unbroken strength.

These are the realities that the International of the congresses believes it can level with Marx's slogans.

22

The worst of these words is called *Communism*. Its critique touches on the cardinal question of *property*. It is not the place here to even outline such a difficult question and to illuminate the deep connections between property and marriage, property and political ideal, property and world-view in all their symbolic force. Here, too, each of the great cultures has its own language. The occidental idea of property is far removed from the ancient, Indian, Chinese ones: *property is power*. What does not have a dynamic effect, all dead possessions, the 'having' in itself counts for little to the genuinely Faustian man. Therein lies the secret of the emphasis on *productive* property above all else, on mere 'ownership'. The sensual ancient joy of accumulated treasures is rare among us. The pride of the conqueror, the merchant and gambler, even the collector of works of art, rests on the consciousness of having acquired *power* with his booty. The Spanish thirst for gold and the English hunger for land are directed towards the acquisition of possessions. Against this energetic concept of property, another rose up in the Renaissance and in Paris: the *pensioner ideal*. Not effect but enjoyment, not 'everything' but 'enough', not action but 'life' was the

ultimate goal of this greed. The *condottieri*[66] wanted their principalities and treasures in order to enjoy the idle culture of their century to
the full. The Medici banking house, one of the first in Europe, was far
from ambitious to dominate the world market. Louis XIV sent out his
generals and tax tenants to create a secure base for the Olympian existence of a Sun Kingdom. The French nobility of Versailles was thoroughly dominated by Renaissance sentiments. Its culture was nothing
less than dynamic. Travelling Englishmen like Young were amazed,
shortly before the Revolution, at how poorly the French nobleman
managed his estates. It was enough for him if he 'had' them and if
the intendant could raise the sums to live in Paris. This aristocracy of
the 18th century formed the strictest contrast to the active, acquiring
and conquering English and Prussian aristocracy. The mere instinct
of self-preservation of French wealth made it incapable of mastering
the world market and of real colonisation even in the great moments
of French history. But the grand seigneur of 1750 is as a type quite the
predecessor of the bourgeois of 1850, that harmless pensioner whom
only national vanity made dangerous from time to time and whose
name Marx really should not have used to designate capitalist society.

For *capital* is the great word in which lies the *English* conception
of property. Capital means economic energy; it is the armour in which
one takes up the struggle for success. Here the French cavalier and
pensioner are opposed by the stock exchange, petroleum and steel
kings, whose enjoyment consists in the consciousness of economic
omnipotence. That a cold can cause prices to fall all over the world,
that a telegram of three words can cause catastrophes on the other
side of the globe, that the trade and industry of whole countries lie
within the sphere of their personal credit, that is their concept of
property, and *private property* at that. One must appreciate the full
pathos of the word. The billionaire demands the unrestricted freedom to change the world situation as he pleases through his private

---

66   The Borgias were Spanish!

decisions, without any ethical standard other than that of success. He fights down the opponent in his field with all the means of credit and speculation. The trust is *his* state, *his* army, and the political state is little more than his agent, whom he commissions with wars, such as the Spanish and South African ones, with treaties and peace agreements. The trustification of the whole world is the ultimate aim of these real master-men: may the nominal property right of the average man remain untouched, may he bequeath, sell, distribute his possessions as *pensioner capital* in full freedom, the economic power of these *possessions as merchant capital* is nevertheless invisibly directed in certain directions from a centre; thus the money magnate is owner in a higher sense and whole peoples and states work under his silent command and according to his omnipresent will. And this concept of property, in which the liberalism of business has disguised itself, is now countered by the Prussian one: property not as private booty, but as the *mandate of the general public*, not as the expression and means of personal power, but as entrusted property, for the administration of which the owner is accountable to the state; national prosperity not as the sum of individual assets, but the individual assets as *functions* of the overall economic power. The great words of Frederick II must always be repeated: 'I am the first *servant* of my state.' When each individual makes this view his own, socialism has become a fact. There is no stronger opposition than Louis XIV with the *fact*: 'The state is me.' Prussianism and Jacobinism, socialist and anarchist instincts, whether on the throne or in the streets, are the strongest opposition conceivable within the West, and on them rests the ineradicable enmity between the two peoples. Napoleon remarked at St. Helena: 'Prussia has been an obstacle to France since the days of Frederick, and will remain so; it has been the greatest obstacle in regard to my intentions for France.'

For indeed, the form in which the revanchist desire of the French working class confronts the propertied classes is the opposite of socialism: Communism in the true sense. The worker also wants to be a pensioner. He hates the leisure of others, which he himself cannot attain in any way. Equality of enjoyment, equal possibility of being a pensioner for everyone is the goal that also underlies Proudhon's famous, genuinely French formula: 'Property is theft.' For here property does not mean power, but *the acquired possibility of enjoyment*. Community of goods and not socialisation of the means of production, distribution of wealth ('all shall belong to all') and not trustification of the value-creating forces — this is a French ideal against an English one. And Fourier's socialist utopia corresponds to this: the dissolution of states into small societies, communes, 'phalansteries', which join together to achieve the richest possible enjoyment of life with the least possible labour.

What the English underclass wants in order to make the property ideal of the ruling upper class accessible to itself, Owen has tried to formulate in a kind of capital reform. But one hardly knows the power of those Viking instincts if one believes that English-American capital will retreat even one step on the road to absolute economic world domination. Unconditional personal freedom and the natural inequality that follows from it on the basis of personal ability is the prerequisite. In place of authoritative socialism, the Anglo-Saxon billionaire sets up a magnificent *private socialism*, a charity and welfare on a grand scale, in which one's own power is once again a pleasure and in which the receiving people are also morally defeated. Over the brilliant way in which these millions are spent, one forgets how they are acquired: it is the attitude of those old corsairs who, at the banquet in a conquered castle, threw the chunks of their table to the prisoners. This *voluntary* surrender of property increases the power of the rest. And whether or not this free act of will is made a legal obligation is basically the point of principle in dispute between the economic parties of the future in England and America. One is prepared today to hand over vast economic areas which do not lend themselves to speculation, such as mining and railways, to the government of a bogus state, but one retains the silent power to make this government itself an executive organ of one's own business through the democratic forms of parliamentarism, that is, by paying for elections and newspapers and thus by recruiting voters and readers. This is the terrible danger of the *enslavement of the world* by mercantilism. Its means today is the League of Nations, that is, a system of peoples possessing 'self-government' in the English manner, that is, in reality, a system of provinces whose populations are exploited by a merchant oligarchy by means of bought parliaments and laws, as the Roman world was by bribing the senators, proconsuls and tribunes of the people.

This becoming system Marx has seen through, and it is against this that all the hatred of his social criticism is directed. He wants to overthrow this *English* concept of omnipotent private property, but he again knows nothing to formulate but a negation: expropriation of the expropriators, robbery of the robbers. And yet this anti-English principle contains the Prussian principle: with full Germanic respect for property, yet assigning the power residing in it not to the individual, but to the totality, to the state. That is called socialisation. With the sure instinct of a government not confused by theories, it has been progressively developed from Frederick William I to Bismarck, from the War and Domain Chambers of the former to the social policy of the latter, until the strict believers and the renegade Marxists of the German Revolution tried to outpace each other in corrupting the idea. Socialisation does *not* mean nationalisation by way of expropriation or theft; it is not a question of nominal ownership at all, but of administrative technique. To buy up enterprises for the sake of the slogan, without measure or aim, and to hand them over, instead of to the initiative and responsibility of their owners, to an administration, which in the end must lose all overview, is to ruin socialism. The old Prussian idea was to subject the entire productive power in its *form* to legislation, while carefully protecting the right of ownership and inheritance, and to let personal enterprise, talent, energy, like the spirit of a practised chess player, work under rules and with *the* freedom which the mastery of the rules affords. This was already the case to a large extent in the old cartels and syndicates, and it should be possible to extend this to the method of working, the evaluation of work, the distribution of profits and the official relations between the ordering and the executing elements. Socialisation means the slow transformation, which will take decades to complete, of the worker into an economic official, of the entrepreneur into a responsible administrative official with very extensive powers, of property into a kind of hereditary fief in the sense of the old times, which is connected with a certain sum of rights and duties. The economic will remains free like the will of the chess player: only the effect takes a regulated course. The Hohenzollerns bred the Prussian civil servant type, the first in the world. It guarantees the possibility of socialisation through its inherited socialist abilities. For 200 years it has been as a method what socialism is as a task. The worker must grow into this type if he ceases to be a Marxist and thus begins to become a socialist. The 'future state' is a bureaucratic state. This is one of the inevitable final states which follow from the presuppositions of our civilisation, which is fixed in its direction. Billionaire socialism, too, would unmistakably transform a people into an army of private civil servants. The great trusts today are already private states, which exercise a protectorate over the official state. Prussian socialism, however, means the *incorporation* of these economic states of the individual professions into the state as a whole. The question of dispute between conservatives and proletarians is basically not at all the necessity of this authoritative-socialist system, which could only be escaped by adopting the American one (the wish of German liberalism), but the question of the supreme command. There are today apparently the possibilities of socialism from above and from below, both in dictatorial form. In reality, both would gradually spill over into the same final form.

At the moment this is still misunderstood to the extent that both parties see the decisive factor in the constitution. But it is not sentences that matter, but personalities. If the workers' leaders do not succeed in bringing out in a short time the high statesmanship required of them, others will take their place. In an organisation which fundamentally abolishes the distinction between workers and civil servants, by opening up to every capable person a regulated career from manual labour of the lowest rank through supervisory offices to the management of an economic body, under the hand of a born statesman conservative and proletarian ultimate aims will come into existence: the complete nationalisation of economic life, not by expropriation but by legislation, will after all coincide. The supreme leadership, however, cannot be republican. Today, if one puts aside all illusions, republic means the venality of the exercising power by private capital. A prince obeys the tradition of his house and the world-view of his profession. Whatever one may think of this: it exempts him from the interest politics of the parties of today. He is their arbiter, and if in a socialistically conceived state the professional councillors up to the highest council of state are a selection according to practical abilities, he can make a narrower selection according to moral qualities. But a president or prime minister or people's representative is the creature of a party, and a party is the creature of those who pay it. A prince is today the only protection of a government against hucksterism. The power of private capital brings together socialist and monarchist principles. The individualist ideal of property means subjection of the state to the free economic powers, which means democracy, which means venality of government by private wealth. In a modern democracy, mass leaders face not the leaders of capital but money itself and its anonymous power. The question is how many of the leaders can resist this power. If you want to know how a democracy that is no longer young and therefore enthusiastic about its own excellence differs in reality from the one that exists in ideological heads, read Sallust[67] on Catilina and Jugurtha. There is

---

67 Sallust (86 BC–35 or 34 BC) was a Roman historian and politician. He praised
    the sunny early days of Rome, in which the state and society were still virtue-
    and glory-oriented. He marks the destruction of Carthage in the Third Punic
    War in 146 BC as the unfortunate turning point, after which any external threat

no doubt that we are facing Roman conditions, but a monarchical-socialist order can render them ineffective.

These are the three ideals of property which are in struggle today: the Communist, the individualist and the socialist, with the ultimate aims of distributing, trustifying and managing all the productive property in the world.

23

Until now I have kept silent about Russia, deliberately, for here not two peoples but *two worlds* are separated. The Russians are not a people at all like the Germans and the English; they contain within themselves the possibility of many peoples of the future, like the Teutons of the Carolingian period. Russianness is the promise of a coming culture, while the evening shadows over the West grow longer and longer. The distinction between Russian and Western spirit cannot be made sharply enough. No matter how deep the spiritual, religious, political and economic differences between the English, the Germans, the Americans and the French may be, in comparison with Russianness they immediately come together to form a unified world. We are deceived by many a Westernised inhabitant of a Russian city. The genuine Russian is as foreign to us inwardly as a Roman of royal times or a Chinese long before Confucius, if they suddenly appeared among us. He himself always knew this when he drew a line between 'Mother Russia' and 'Europe'.

For us, the Russian primal soul — behind dirt, music, brandy, humility and strange sadness — is something unfathomable. Our judgements, those of late, urban and spiritually matured people of a very different culture, are formed by us. What we 'recognise' there is not this just dawning soul, of which even Dostoevsky speaks only in helpless tones, but our *mental image* of it, which is determined by

---

to Rome came to an abrupt end, and, as a result, the good old moral values lost power and prestige in society. — *Transl.*

the surface image of Russian life and Russian history and falsified by our relationship words such as will, reason, mind, drawn from our own inner experience. Nevertheless, some of us may be able to form an impression of it that can hardly be put into words, and which at least leaves no doubt about the immense gulf that lies between it and ourselves.

This childishly dull and foreboding Russianness has now been tormented, disturbed, wounded, poisoned from 'Europe' by the imposed forms of an already manly perfected, alien and imperious culture. Cities of our kind, with the pretensions of our spiritual attitude, were drilled into the flesh of this people, overripe ways of thinking, views of life, ideas of state, sciences were inculcated into the undeveloped consciousness. Around 1700, Peter the Great imposed on the people the political Baroque style with cabinet diplomacy, power politics, administration and army according to the Western model; around 1800, English ideas, which were quite incomprehensible to these people, came over in the version of French writers to confuse the minds of the thin upper class; even before 1900, the bookworms of the Russian intelligentsia introduced Marxism, an extremely complicated product of Western European dialectics, of whose background they had not the slightest idea. Peter the Great transformed the genuine Russian tsardom into a great power in the Western system of states, thus corrupting its natural development, and the 'intelligentsia', itself a piece of the genuine Russian spirit corrupted in these alien cities, distorted the primitive thinking of the country, with its dark longing for own, distant future designs such as the common ownership of land of 'Mother Russia', into childish and empty theories in the taste of French professional revolutionaries. Petrinism and Bolshevism have transformed equally senseless and fatally misunderstood creations of the West, such as the Court of Versailles and the Paris Commune, into strong realities thanks to infinite Russian humility and sacrificial joy. Yet their institutions cling to the surface of Russian being, and one as well as the other is subject to the constant possibility of sudden disappearance and equally sudden return. Russianness itself has so far had only religious experiences, none truly social and political. One misjudges Dostoevsky, a saint in the perverse and ridiculous guise of a novelist forced from the West, if one conceives of his social 'problems' differently from his novel form. His real essence is more between the lines than in them, and in *The Brothers Karamazov* it rises to a religious depth beside which only Dante may be mentioned. Revolutionary politics, however, come only from a small stratum of the great cities, which no longer feels securely Russian and is hardly Russian in origin, and therefore moves in the forms of doctrinaire coercion on the one hand and instinctive resistance on the other.

And hence that terrible, deep, primordial Russian hatred of the West, the poison in one's own body, which speaks with the same strength from Dostoevsky's inner suffering and Tolstoy's loud outbursts as from the wordless feelings of the little man; the often unconscious, often hidden behind a sincere love, insatiable hatred of *all* symbols of Faustian will, of the cities, Petersburg first, which have nested themselves as bases of this will in the peasantry of these endless plains, of science and the arts, of thinking, feeling, the state, law, administration, of money, industry, education, society, of everything. It *is the primal hatred of the apocalypse against ancient culture*, and something of the sinister bitterness of Maccabean times, and much later still of that uprising which led to the destruction of Jerusalem, surely underlies all Bolshevism. Its doctrinal constructions would not have produced the force with which the movement continues today. With the instincts of *subterranean* Russia it pushes against the West, which first presented itself in Petrinism, and it will be destroyed in the end, as a product of this Petrinism, in order to complete the inner liberation from 'Europe'.

The Western proletarian wants to transform the civilisation of the West in his own sense; the Russian *intelligentsia* wants to destroy it, mostly against its knowledge, which floats thinly on the surface of its instincts. *This* is the meaning of Eastern *nihilism*. Our civilisation has long since become a purely urban one, but there is no 'mass' there, only a *'people'*. The genuine Russian is a peasant without distinction, even as a scholar, even as a civil servant. These imitation cities with their imitation masses and mass ideology do not touch his interest. In spite of all Marxism, there is only one land question. The 'worker' is a misunderstanding. The untouched, undestroyed land is the only reality, as it was with the Germanic peoples of the Carolingian period. We went through this stage a millennium ago. We do not understand each other. We Western Europeans can no longer live in connection with the original soil. When we go to the country, we carry the city with us, along with all its mental conditions, in our blood, not only in our heads like the Russian intelligentsia. But the Russian inwardly carries his village into these Russian cities. One must always distinguish the Russian soul from the Russian system, the consciousness of the leaders from the instincts of the led, in order not to misjudge the unbridgeable gap between Eastern and Western 'socialism'. What is Pan-Slavism but a Western political mask for the feeling of a great religious mission? The Russian worker, in spite of all the industrial slogans of surplus value and expropriation, is not a metropolitan worker, not a mass man like those in Manchester, Essen and Pittsburg, but a runaway ploughman and mower with a hatred of the foreign distant power which has corrupted him for his profession, from which the soul cannot, after all, detach itself. It is quite indifferent what kind of views Bolshevism works with. If its programmes contained the opposite of everything, its unconscious mission for the awakening Russia would still be the same: nihilism.

But the intellectual elite of *our* cities is enthusiastic about it. It has become a fashion of idle and broken brains, a weapon of rotting metropolitan souls, an expression of putrid blood. The Spartacism of the salons belongs together with theosophy and occultism: it means to us what the cult of Isis was not to the Oriental slaves of Rome but to degenerate Romans themselves. That it has moved into Berlin is connected with the monstrous lie of this revolution, in which nothing real was left. That barren fools founded peasant councils here to ape the formulas of the Soviets, that one did not notice how the land question was *the* problem there, the city question here, means little. In Germany, Spartacism has no future vis-à-vis socialism. But Bolshevism will conquer *Paris* and there, in fusion with anarchic syndicalism, satisfy the tired French soul in need of sensation. It will be the form in which the *taedium vitae*[68] of this life-saturated giant city expresses itself. As a dangerous poison for refined minds, it has a greater future in the West than in the East.

In Russia, the only possible form for a nation under these conditions will be a new tsarism of some kind, and it can be assumed that this will be closer to Prussian socialist forms than to parliamentary capitalist ones. The future of subterranean Russia, however, lies not in the solution of political or social problems, but *in the birth of a new religion*, the third, out of the rich possibilities of Christianity, just as the Germanic-Western culture began around the year 1000 with the unconscious creation of the second. Dostoevsky is one of the forerunners of this faith, still nameless but already penetrating with a silent, infinitely tender violence.

We people of the West are religiously finished. In our urban souls, early religiosity has long since intellectualised itself into 'problems'. The Church is completed with the Council of Trent. Puritanism has become capitalism, pietism has become socialism. The Anglo-American sects represent only the need of nervous businessmen for an occupation of the mind with theological questions. Nothing can be more pathetic than the attempts of a certain Protestantism to rub its corpse alive again with Bolshevik excrement. Elsewhere the same has been attempted with occultism and theosophy. And nothing is more deceptive than the hope that the Russian religion of the future will fertilise the Western one. There should be no doubt about this today: Russian nihilism, with its hatred of the state, knowledge, art,

---

68   Latin: a feeling of being tired of life. — *Transl.*

is *also* directed against Rome and Wittenberg, whose spirit has expressed itself in *all* forms of Western culture and is to be met in them. Russianness will push this development aside and, via Byzantium, link up again directly with Jerusalem.

But this says once again how insignificant Bolshevism, this bloody caricature of Western problems, which for their part once arose out of Western religiosity, is for the great world question which the West *today* poses for decision and which is posed only for *superficial* Russia: the choice between Prussian or English ideas, socialism or capitalism, state or parliament.

Let me summarise. What has been said in these brief remarks should give that part of our people which, through energy, self-discipline and spiritual superiority, is called to lead the next generation a picture of the times in which we stand and the direction in which our destiny points us.

We now know what is at stake: not the fate of Germany alone, but the fate of the entire civilisation. It is the decisive question not only for Germany but for the *world*, and it must be solved in Germany *for* the world: in the future, shall commerce govern the state or the state govern commerce?

Prussianism and socialism are the same thing to it. Up to now we have not seen that. We still do not see it today. Marx's teaching and class selfishness have been to blame for the fact that *both*, the socialist working class and the conservative element, have misunderstood each other and thus misunderstood socialism.

Today, however, the equality of purpose can no longer be mistaken. Prussianism and Socialism stand *together against the inner England*, against the world outlook which pervades, paralyses and disinherits our whole life as a people. The danger is immense. Woe to those who are absent in this hour out of selfishness and lack of understanding! They will ruin others and themselves. Unification means the fulfilment of the Hohenzollern idea and *at the same time* the redemption of the workers. *There is salvation only for both or for none.*

The working class must free itself from the illusions of Marxism. Marx is dead. Socialism as a form of existence is at its beginning, but socialism as a special movement of the German proletariat is at its end. *For the worker there is only Prussian socialism or nothing.*

The conservatives must free themselves from the selfishness for the sake of which the Great Elector[69] laid the head at the feet of Captain von Kalckstein. Democracy, however one may value it, is the form of this century that *will* prevail. For the state, there is only democratisation or nothing. For the conservatives, there is only conscious socialism or annihilation. But we need liberation from the forms of Anglo-French democracy. We have one of our own.

The meaning of socialism is that it is not the opposition of rich and poor, but the rank that achievement and ability give, that governs life. This is *our* freedom, freedom from the economic arbitrariness of the individual.

What I hope is that no one remains in the depths who was born to command by his abilities, that no one commands who was not called to do so by his talents. Socialism means ability, not will. It is not the rank of intentions but the rank of achievements that is decisive. I address the youth. I call on all those who have marrow in their bones and blood in their veins. Educate yourselves! Become men! We do not need any more ideologues, no more talk of education and cosmopolitanism and the spiritual mission of the Germans. We need toughness; we need a brave scepticism; we need a class of socialist gentlemen. Once again: socialism means power, power and always power. Plans and thoughts are nothing without power. The road to power is marked out: the valuable part of the German working class in conjunction with

---

69 Frederick William (1620–1688), Margrave of Brandenburg and Duke of Prussia, laid the foundations for the later great power of Prussia with his reforms. He took office during the Thirty Years' War in a depopulated and devastated country. His victory over the Swedes at the Battle of Fehrbellin on 18 June 1675 earned him the nickname of the Great Elector. He established a standing army, brought 15,000 Protestants to Prussia, founded universities and had canals and roads built. — *Transl.*

the best bearers of the old Prussian sense of state, both determined to found a strictly socialist state, to democratise in the *Prussian* sense, both forged together by a unity of the sense of duty, by the consciousness of a great task, by the will to obey in order to rule, to die in order to conquer, by the strength to make tremendous sacrifices in order to enforce what we were born to do, *what we are*, what would not be there without us.

We are socialists. *We do not want to have been so for nothing.*

RUSSIA'S DOUBLE FACE AND THE GERMAN PROBLEMS IN THE EAST

BY OSWALD SPENGLER

LECTURE GIVEN ON 14 FEBRUARY 1922 AT THE RHENISH-WESTPHALIAN ECONOMIC CONFERENCE IN ESSEN.

IN VIEW OF the desperate situation of Germany, which, defenceless and ruled by the friends of its enemies from the West, has to endure the unabated war by economic and diplomatic means, the great problems of the East, political and economic, rise to quite decisive importance. If one wants to understand the real, very complicated situation on this side, it is not enough to know the present conditions of the vast area, the Russian domestic policy and economic organisation of these days, and the geographical and military conditions under which Soviet Russia lives. One must understand the world-historical fact *of Russianness in general*, its position and development between the great, old cultures — the West, China, India and Islam — and in the course of the centuries, its people, its soul. Political and economic life is life in general and is an expression, a form, a part of this life, even in the seemingly most sober questions of the day.

One can try to look at these things with 'Russian' eyes, as our Communist and democratic writers and party people do, that is, from the social ideologies of the West. But that is not Russian, even if there are still so many city people in Russia today who think so themselves. Or with Western European ones, by judging the Russian people like any other people of 'Europe'. But this is just as wrong. In reality, the real Russian is very foreign to us in soul, as foreign as the Indian and Chinese, with whom one also never looks down to the bottom of the soul. 'Russia and Europe', as the Russians very correctly distinguish, the 'motherland' of Russia against the 'fatherland' of Western peoples, are two worlds that are very far from each other. The Russian understands this foreignness. Unless he is of mixed blood, he never gets beyond a shy aversion or naive admiration towards the German, the French and the English. The Tatar and Turk are more understandable and closer to him in his expressions of life. We allow ourselves to be seduced by the *geographical* concept of 'Europe', which has only arisen from *printed maps* since 1500, but the real Europe stops at the Vistula. The activity of the German knightly orders in the Baltic region was colonisation in a foreign part of the world and has never been understood differently by its participants.

If we want to understand this strange people, we have to look back at our own past. Russian history from 900 to 1900 does not correspond to that of the West in these centuries, but to that from Roman times to Charlemagne and the Staufen emperors. Our heroic poetry from Arminius to the Song of Hildebrand, the Song of Roland and the Song of the Nibelungs is repeated in the Russian *byliny*, folk songs that begin with the knights at the court of Prince Vladimir († 1015), with Igor's military expedition and Ilya of Murom and have remained fruitful and alive through Ivan the Terrible, Peter the Great and the fire of Moscow up to the present day. But a very different primal feeling speaks from these two worlds of the most original poetry. Russian life has a different sense. The endless plain created a softer people, humble and melancholy, also mentally absorbed in the flat expanse, without any real personal will, inclined to submission. This is the prerequisite of the great politics from Genghis Khan to Lenin. The Russians are also semi-nomads, *even today*. Even the rule of the Soviets will not succeed in preventing the factory workers from roaming from one factory to another, without need, merely out of the longing to wander[1]. That is why the thoroughly educated skilled worker is so rare in Russia[2]. For the peasant, too, his home is not the village, the landscape of his birth, but the vast Russian plain. Even the *mir*, the so-called agrarian communism, which is nothing ancient but arose from the administrative technique of tax collection of tsarist governments, has not been able to bind the peasants spiritually to the soil like the Germanic peasants. They flocked by the thousands to the newly developed areas of the southern Russian steppes, Caucasia and Turkestan to satisfy their feelings and their search for the limits of the infinite. This move is matched by the ceaseless expansion of the empire to the natural limits of the sea and high mountains. In the 16th century, Siberia was occupied and settled as far as Lake Baikal, and in the 17th as far as the Pacific Ocean.

Even deeper, however, lies a dark mystical pull towards Byzantium, towards Jerusalem, which dresses itself in the forms of Orthodox Christianity and numerous sects and has thus been a power even within great politics, but in which an unborn new religion of a still immature people slumbers. All this has nothing of the West, for Poles and Balkan Slavs are also 'Asiatics'. And economically, too, this people lived in its own, entirely 'non-European' forms. The merchant family of the Stroganovs, who under Ivan Grozny[3] began the conquest

---

1   Cf. many stories by Leskov and especially by Gorky.

2   Except perhaps in the earlier artels, groups of workers under self-elected leaders who hired themselves out to do certain jobs in factories and on estates. Good description of an artel in Leskov's 'The Sealed Angel'.

3   Grozny means the fearsome, the just, the awe-inspiring, in an *appreciative* sense, not the 'terrible' with a Western European undertone. Ivan IV was a creator like Peter the Great, one of the most important rulers of all time.

of Siberia on their own account and provided the Tsar with their own regiments, has nothing to do with great businessmen of the same century in the West. Thus, the vast country with its wandering people could have lasted for centuries and waited for its future, for the time being as an object of Western colonial aspirations, had it not been for the appearance of a man of immense world political importance — Peter the Great.

A change in the fate of an entire people, such as he accomplished, can perhaps not be proven a second time in all of history with such consequences. His will took Russia out of the Asiatic context and made it a Western-style state within the Western world of states. He wanted to lead Russia, until then a landlocked country, to the sea, first in vain to the Sea of Azov, then with lasting success to the Baltic. The fact that the coast of the Pacific Ocean has already been reached is of no importance to him. The Baltic coast is his bridge to 'Europe'. There he founded Petersburg, with its German name a symbol. Instead of the old Russian markets and residences like Kiev, Moscow and Nizhny Novgorod, Western European cities are planted in the Russian landscape. The administration, the legislation, the state are being built up according to foreign patterns. A feudal nobility like that in England and France is being created from the boyar dynasties of old Russian chieftains. A high society is to be created above the rural people, according to dress, custom, language and thought. In fact, an upper class with a light Western varnish soon forms in the cities. People play at scholarship like the Germans and have *esprit* and manners like the French. The entire rationalism of Western Europe invades, barely understood, undigested, disastrous, and already Catherine II, a German, finds herself compelled to send writers of the ilk of Novikov and Radishchev to prison and banishment because they wanted to test the ideas of the Enlightenment on Russianness and its political and religious forms[4].

---

4   'Jehovah, Jupiter, Brahma, God of Abraham, God of Moses, God of Confucius,
    God of Zoroaster, God of Socrates, God of Marcus Aurelius, God of the

And likewise the economy becomes different. Alongside the age-old Russian river navigation, sea trade to distant ports is taking its place. The commercial habits of the Stroganovs, for example, with their caravan trade to China, and the Nizhny Novgorod trade fair, were replaced by Western European 'thinking in money' with banks and stock exchanges. Alongside the old crafts and mining in the Urals, which was carried out in a completely primeval way, appeared factories, machines, and finally railways and steamships.

Above all, however, a Western-style policy emerged, based on an army that was no longer formed out of the conditions of the struggle against Tatars, Turks and Kirghiz, but for the struggle against Western armies on Western soil, and which, by its very existence, repeatedly seduced Petersburg diplomacy into seeing political problems in the West alone.

Despite all the weaknesses of an artificial creation out of recalcitrant material, Petrinism was something mighty in the 200 years of its existence. What it had built up can only be appreciated from a distant future and assessed by the heap of rubble it left behind. He apparently extended 'Europe' at least as far as the Urals and made it a unity of culture. An empire that reached as far as the Bering Strait and the Hindukush was subjected to 'European' morality to such an extent that the difference between cities in Ireland and Portugal, for example, and those in Turkestan or the Caucasus no longer mattered around 1900. People travelled more safely and comfortably in Siberia than in many countries of Western Europe. The Siberian railway was the last triumph, the last symbol of Petrine will before the collapse.

But this mighty exterior covered the doom within. Petrinism was and remained a *foreign body* in Russianness. There was in reality not one Russia, but two, the apparent and the true, the official and the subterranean. And the foreign element carried in the poison from which the mighty body ailed and died. It was the spirit of Western

Christians, you are the same everywhere, Eternal One!' (Radishchev).

rationalism in the 18th century and of materialism in the 19th century, inaccessible and incomprehensible to genuine Russian thought, which led its grimacing and dangerous existence as Russian nihilism among the 'intelligentsia' of the cities. A type of intelligent Russian emerged who, like the Reform Turk, Reform Chinese and Reform Indian, is mentally and spiritually flattened, emptied, corrupted by Western Europe to the point of cynicism. It began with Voltaire and led via Proudhon and Marx to Spencer and Häckel. It was precisely the upper class of Tolstoy's time that played at it, blasé, wanting to be witty, faithless, hostile to tradition, and this world-view penetrated down to the yeast of the big cities, the literati, popular agitators and students who 'went to the people' and there developed a hatred of the Western-style upper class: The result was doctrinaire Bolshevism.

At first, however, it was exclusively Russian foreign policy that was noticed, and palpably noticed, in the West. The original Russian nation was not seen and, at any rate, not understood. It was a harmless ethnographic curiosity that was occasionally imitated at masquerade balls and in operettas. For us, Russia was a great power in the Western sense, which played the game of great politics energetically, sometimes in a leading role.

Here, however, two currents, alien and hostile to each other, were mixed up: the ancient, instinctive, unclear, unconscious, subterranean one that is present in the soul of every Russian, no matter how Westernised his consciousness may be — the mystical pull towards the south, towards Constantinople and Jerusalem, a genuine crusading mood, such as was in the blood of our Gothic ancestors and which we can hardly feel today. And on top of this was the official foreign policy of the diplomacy of a great power: Petersburg against Moscow! There is the need to play a role in the great world, to be recognised and treated as an equal in 'Europe'. Hence the super-polite form, the excellent manners, the impeccable taste, all of which had already been in decline in Paris since Napoleon III. The finest tone of Western European society was learned in some *Petersburg* circles. Yet this kind of Russian loved none of the Western European peoples. They were admired, esteemed, ridiculed and despised, as the case may be, but they were treated practically only in terms of the advantage or disadvantage that Russia derived from them. This is the basis of the respect shown in the wars of liberation for Prussia, which was gladly taken, and in the years before the World War for France, at whose senile cries of revanche one laughed. For the intelligent and ambitious upper classes, however, Russia was the future master of Europe, intellectually *and politically*. Even Napoleon felt this. The Russian Army was positioned on the western frontier, in Western proportions and thoroughly trained for western terrain and Western opponents. The defeat by Japan in 1905 was partly due to the lack of training for any other theatre of war. This policy was served by the system of ambassadorial posts in the great capitals of the West, which the Soviet government replaced with the agitation centres of Communist parties. The Great Catherine took away Poland, removing the last barrier between East and West. This policy reached its peak with the symbolic entry of Alexander I, the 'saviour of Europe', into Paris. At the Congress of Vienna, Russia was at times decisive, as it was in the Holy Alliance, which Metternich established as the bulwark of tradition against the Western revolution and which, as late as 1849, prompted Nicholas I to establish order in the Habsburg state in the interests of its government. Thus, through the successful tradition of Petersburg diplomacy, Russia became ever more deeply involved in the great politics of Western Europe. It took part in all the intrigues and combinations which were not only remote from Russianism but completely incomprehensible to it. The army on the Western frontier was made numerically the strongest in the world, for no internal reason, for Russia was the only country which no one had intended to attack since Napoleon, while Germany was threatened by France and Russia, Italy by France and Austria, Austria by France and Russia. An alliance was sought with it in order to be able to put the Russian Army on its side as a weight in the balance and thus stimulated the ambition of Russian society to ever greater efforts for non-Russian interests. We all grew up under the impression that Russia was a great European power and that the land beyond the Volga was colonial territory. The centre of gravity of the empire was necessarily west of Moscow, not in the Volga region. But the educated Russian thought so himself. He felt that the defeat in the Far East of 1905 was only a trivial colonial adventure, while he felt that the slightest defeat on the western frontier was a disgrace — in the eyes of the West. In the south and north, a fleet was built that was completely superfluous for coastal defence and merely intended to play a role in the great politics of the West.

But the Turkish wars to 'liberate' the Christian Balkan peoples already touched the Russian soul more deeply. Russia as the heir of Turkey — that was a mystical thought. There was no diplomatic disagreement about that. That was the will of God. Only the Turkish wars were truly popular. Alexander I feared assassination by an officer conspiracy in 1807, not without reason. The entire officer corps wanted war against Turkey instead of Napoleon. This led to Alexander's alliance with Napoleon in Tilsit, which dominated world politics until 1812. It is significant how Dostoevsky, unlike Tolstoy, was ecstatic by the war of 1877. He came alive, incessantly writing down his metaphysical visions and preaching the religious mission of Russianness against Byzantium. The *Russian Messenger*, however, refused to print the last part of *Anna Karenina* because they did not dare offer Tolstoy's scepticism to the public.

As already mentioned, the educated, unbelieving, Western-thinking Russian also had within him the general mystical pull towards Jerusalem: the '*Third* Rome' of the monk of Kiev, which was to bring the fulfilment of Christ's message through holy Russia to the Jerusalem of the apostles after the Rome of the popes and the Wittenberg of Luther. This barely conscious national instinct of *all* Russians rebelled against any power that threatened to politically shift the path to Jerusalem via Byzantium. Whereas everywhere else national vanity — in the West — or indifference — in the Far East — was hurt or only touched, here the mystical soul of the people was struck and deeply aroused. Hence the great successes of the Slavophile movement, which basically sought to win over neither Poles nor Czechs, but only the Slavs of the Christian Balkans, the neighbours of Constantinople. Even earlier, the holy war against Napoleon and the burning of Moscow was a matter of nationalism, not actually because of the violation and plundering of Russian territory, but because of Napoleon's plans to dominate the Adriatic Sea by taking away the Illyrian provinces (today's Yugoslavia) in 1809 and thereby decisively strengthen his influence over Turkey—against Russia—in order to pave the way to India from here or from Moscow through his connection with it and Persia. The hatred of Napoleon then transferred to the Habsburg monarchy when the latter's intentions on Turkish territory—since Metternich on the Danube estuaries, since 1878 on Salonika—put the Russian tendency in danger. It extended to England since the Crimean War, when it also seemed to claim the Turkish inheritance by blocking the straits and later occupying Egypt and Cyprus.

And finally Germany became the object of this deep hatred, which could not be influenced by practical considerations, when, since 1878, it turned from an ally more and more into the protector and upholder of the decaying Habsburg state and thus, unfortunately, in spite of Bismarck's warning, also of its plans in the Balkans, and even lastly did not understand the idea of Count Witte, the last German-friendly diplomat, to choose between Austria and Russia. But it could have won Russia back as a sincere ally as soon as it gave up its close ties with Austria. As late as 1911, a reorientation of Germany's entire policy might have been possible.

This hatred of Germany began to spread throughout Russian society after the Berlin Congress, when Bismarck succeeded in keeping Russia's diplomacy in check in the interest of world peace and the maintenance of the balance of the 'European' great powers. Seen from Germany, it was probably the right thing to do at the time, and in any case a masterpiece of Bismarckian statesmanship; in the eyes of Petersburg, however, it was a mistake: it deprived the Russian soul of hope for the Turkish inheritance in favour of England and Austria. This *soul* belonged to the imponderables inaccessible to diplomatic considerations. Hostility grew and seized all strata of the Russian cities. It was temporarily deflected when Russia was forced to see and experience the Far East as a danger zone by the very sudden appearance of Japanese power, which brought the whole of world politics into another system. But this was soon forgotten, above all as a result of the grotesque clumsiness of German politics, which understood nothing, neither situations nor possibilities, until the nonsensical idea of Berlin-Baghdad emerged and Germany thus seemed to want to master this route via Constantinople itself, which was equally worthless for its politics and economy.

Similarly, in Russia's economic life, two currents lay one above the other, the upper one attacking and penetrating, while the other was suffering in the true sense of the word. This was the old Russian peasantry with its early 'agriculture', to which the old Russian merchant with his fairs, freights, Volga ships belonged, and likewise the Russian crafts and the primitive mining in the Urals, which developed quite independently of Western methods and experiences from the ancient methods of pre-Christian 'forging peoples'. For it was here that the forging of iron was invented in the 2nd millennium BC, of which the Greeks still had a dim idea. Above this, however, the civilised world of Western metropolitan economy with its banks, stock exchanges, factories and railways spread ever more powerfully: money economy against goods economy, both of which rubbed against each other, hated or despised each other, attacked and sought to destroy each other. But the Petrine state needed the money economy to pay for its great Western-style politics, its army, its administration with its primitive corruption, a public custom that belongs mentally to the goods economy and is in essence something quite different from the secret corruption of, say, Western European parliamentarians. The state protected and strengthened the Western capitalist-directed economic thinking that was neither created nor understood by Russianness, but was merely introduced and endured — *with its doctrinaire inversion, the Communist economic doctrine* inseparable from it, the Marxist capitalism of the underclass preached in the Petrine cities as an unclear gospel by students and agitators to the dull masses.

But it was not this doctrinaire, literary current in the underground of the big cities that was the decisive thing for the future, the really inciting thing, but the deep, instinctively religious aversion to Western economic forms in general. One felt that 'money' and *all* economic forms ruled by it, capitalist *and* socialist, were sinful and satanic, a genuine feeling that in the West in the Gothic centuries rebelled against the economic practice of the Arab-Jewish world and led to the prohibition of the taking of interest for the Christian. For centuries this has become an empty phrase of pulpits and prayer halls in the West, while in Russia it has just now become a spiritual problem. This drove numerous Russians to suicide out of 'fear of surplus value' because, out of their primitive feeling and thinking, they could not imagine any kind of acquisition through which other 'fellow human beings' were not 'exploited'. This Russian thinking saw in the world of capitalism an enemy, a poison, the great sin which it attributed to the Petrine state, regardless of the deep veneration for the little father Tsar.

So deep and manifold are the roots from which the Russian worldview of intellectual nihilism arose, roughly since the Crimean War, and as its last fruit, Bolshevism, which destroyed the Petrine system in 1917 and replaced it with something that would be utterly impossible in the West. There is in it the hatred of the strict Slavophiles against Petersburg and its spirit[5], the hatred of the peasants against the *mir*, against village communism, which contradicted the general peasant instinct of property, arising from the fact of the family lasting

---

5 'The first condition of the liberation of Russian popular feeling is to hate Petersburg with all one's heart and soul' (Aksakov to Dostoevsky).

generations, the hatred of all against capitalism, against the whole industrial economy, the machines, the railways, the state and the army, which protected this cynical world against the outbreak of Russian instincts, a very primeval, religious hatred of misunderstood powers perceived as godless, which one does not want to transform but to destroy, so that one's own life may resume its old course.

The peasants despised the *intelligentsia* and their agitation as much as what they were agitating against, but for the time being this agitation has led a small swarm of clever and largely inferior people to rule. Lenin's creation, too, is Western, is Petersburg, is alien, hostile and odious to the great majority of Russians, and it will in some way one day pass away. It is a revolt against the West out of Western thinking. It therefore seeks to preserve the economic forms of industrial labour and capitalist speculation as well as the authoritarian state, only that in place of the tsarist government and private capitalist economic forms, it substitutes the government of a group and state capitalism, which calls itself Communism for the sake of doctrine.

It is a new victory of Petersburg over Moscow *and no doubt the last*, the final self-destruction of Petrinism from below. The real victim is precisely the element that hoped to be liberated by the overthrow: the genuine Russian, the peasant and artisan, the believer. Western revolutions, the English and the French, want to improve something that has grown through theories and therefore never succeed. Here, however, a whole world was dissolved into nothing without resistance. Only the artificiality of Peter the Great's creation explains why a small group of revolutionaries, almost without exception fools and cowards, had such an effect: it was a beautiful pretence that suddenly crumbled.

The Bolshevism of the first years thus has a double meaning. It destroys an artificial entity alien to the people, of which it itself remains for the time being as an appurtenant remnant. Beyond that, however, it clears the way for a new culture that will awaken at some point between 'Europe' and East Asia. It is more a beginning than an end. It is temporary, superficial, alien only insofar as it is the self-destruction of the Petrine creation, the grotesque attempt to turn this social superstructure into its opposite according to the theories of Karl Marx. In the depths lies the Russian peasantry, which undoubtedly played a greater part in the success of the revolution of 1917 than is admitted by the intellectual rabble, the believing peasantry, which, without knowing it clearly today, is the mortal enemy of Bolshevism and is oppressed by it worse than by the Mongols and the old tsars, and yet, precisely through this, will attain to the consciousness of its quite differently directed will. It is the people of the future, which cannot be stifled and falsified, which will undoubtedly, however slowly, replace, transform, dominate or destroy Bolshevism in its present form. How this will happen, no one can know today. It depends, among other things, on the appearance or absence of decisive men who, like Genghis Khan, Ivan IV, Peter the Great and Lenin, take fate into their iron hands. Here, too, Dostoevsky stands against Tolstoy: he is the future against the present. Dostoevsky was decried as a reactionary because he did not even see the nihilistic problems in his *Demons*. For him, such things were only part of the Petrine system. But Tolstoy, the man of good society, lived in this element; he also represented it through his revolt, a protest in Western form against the West. Tolstoy, not Marx, is the real guide to Bolshevism. Dostoevsky is its future overcomer.

There is no doubt that a new nation is in the making, one whose spiritual existence is shaken and threatened by a terrible fate, one that will be forced to resist and will strengthen and flourish, one that is passionately religious in a way that we Western Europeans have not been and cannot be for centuries, with a tremendous power of expansion as soon as this religious urge is directed towards a goal. Such a nation does not count the sacrifices that die for an idea, as we do, because it is young, strong and fertile. The deep veneration enjoyed in recent centuries by the 'holy peasants', whom the government usually banished to Siberia or otherwise made disappear — figures like the priest John of Kronstadt, even Rasputin, but also Ivan and Peter the Great —, will awaken a type of new leaders, leaders for crusades and fairy-tale conquests. The world around is tired enough, torn, religiously yearning without being religiously fruitful, to suddenly take on a different face under certain circumstances. Perhaps Bolshevism itself will change in this sense under new leaders; it is not likely. For this ruling horde — a community like once the Mongols of the Golden Horde — always looks to the West, with the gaze of Peter the Great, who also took the homeland of his thoughts as the goal of his politics. But the silent Russianness of the deep has already forgotten the West and has long since looked towards the Near East and East Asia, a people of the great inland plains, not of the seas.

The interest in Western questions is maintained only by the ruling stratum, which organises and supports the Communist parties in the various countries, I believe, without any prospect of success. It is the mere consequence of Marxist doctrine, not an enterprise of practical statesmanship. Only through serious political mistakes in foreign policy, for example, that of Germany, could Russia's gaze be turned again — disastrously for *both* parts — towards the West, for example, through a 'crusade' of the Western powers against Bolshevism, naturally in the service of French-English finance capital. The silent movement of Russia is towards Jerusalem and Inner Asia, and *the* enemy will always be the one blocking these roads. The fact that England founded the Baltic States and placed them under her influence, that Russia lost the Baltic Sea, does not have a deep effect. Petersburg has been abandoned, a ruined city from the time of Petrinism. The old Moscow is once again the centre of the country. But the destruction of Turkey and its division into spheres of influence of France and England, the founding of the Little Entente by France, which closes off and threatens the south from Romania, the French attempts to dominate the Danube line and the Black Sea by reconstructing the Habsburg state in some form under French leadership, make England and above all France the heirs of Russian hatred. It is the revival of Napoleonic tendencies, and the Berezina may not have been the last event of great symbolism in that direction. Byzantium is and remains the sacred gateway of future Russian politics, just as, on the other hand, Inner Asia is no longer a conquered land but a part of the sacred soil of Russian nationhood.

German policy towards this rapidly changing, growing Russia demands all the tactical skill of a great statesman and connoisseur of this very side, whom I do not see today. That we are not the enemies of Russia is self-evident, but whose friend are we to be — that of the Russia of today or tomorrow? Is both possible, or does one exclude the other? Will not a new enmity grow out of careless alliances?

And our economic relations, both actual and possible in the future, are just as dark and difficult. Politics and economics are two very different spheres of life, completely different in thought, method, aim and spiritual significance, which is not recognised in the age of practical materialism and yet is to a fatal degree correct. The economy is *the object of politics*, necessarily the second, not the first element of history. The tendencies of present and future Russian economic life, which is dominated only on the surface by state capitalism and in the depths by almost religious conceptions, and which is to be strictly distinguished from great politics, are difficult to see through and still more difficult to treat correctly from abroad. The Russia of the last tsars was outwardly and apparently an economic entity of a thoroughly Western European type, and the Bolshevik one would like to be so, would even like to be a model of the West in its Communist style. In fact, from the point of view of the Western economy, it is an immense colonial area in which the Russian of the countryside and the small towns is essentially peasant and artisanal. Industry and the movement of goods from it through the railway network and the sale of goods through wholesale trade is and remains inwardly alien to him. *The economic organiser, the factory manager, the engineer and inventor are not 'Russian' types.* The genuine Russian will allow the foreigner what he forbids himself, what he is inwardly incapable of doing — namely, as a people, as much as the individual tries to adapt himself to the forms of the modern world economy. An in-depth comparison with the time of the Crusades will make clear what I mean. At that time, too, the young peoples of the North were economically alienated from the cities, living only agriculturally — even in the small towns; castle towns and residences that were economically only *markets*. The Jews and Arabs were 'older' by a millennium and therefore sat in their ghettos as connoisseurs of a metropolitan money economy. The Western European has quite the same position in today's Russia.

The machine industry is, in its spirit, un-Russian and will always be perceived by the Russian as alien, as sinful, as diabolical. He tolerates it, he can even appreciate it as a means to greater ends, like the Japanese, for one casts out the devil with Beelzebub, but he is not spiritually absorbed in it, like the Germanic nations, who created it out of their dynamic world feeling as a sign and means of their struggling existence. This industry will always be essentially in the hands or under the direction of foreigners — but the Russian will know very sensitively how to distinguish whether it is for his benefit or for the benefit of others.

As far as 'money' is concerned, for the Russians the cities are markets for the rural transport of goods; for us they have been centres for the dynamics of money since the 18th century. Economic 'thinking in money' will be impossible for the Russian for a long time to come, and in this respect, as I have said, Russia is a colony from the point of view of foreign economy. Germany will be able to draw advantages from her neighbourhood, especially under the impression that both powers have the same opponent, the high finance of the Entente states.

But the German economy will not be able to open up all these possibilities without cover from a superior policy. Without this cover, only an *overexploitation of opportunities* will develop, which will leave a bad legacy for the future. France's policy has undoubtedly been short-sighted and purely destructive for centuries and is determined by the sadistic character of the people. A German policy, however, which could be seriously considered, does not exist at all.

It is therefore the first task of German economic leadership to help put German domestic policy in order, and thereby to create the *prerequisite* for a foreign policy which recognises and fulfils its tasks. This task has not yet been recognised for its immense importance, especially for the economy. It is not a question, in keeping with the common prejudice, of classifying politics according to the current interests of individual groups, as has been done up to now with the help of the most inferior politics there is, party politics. It is not a question of advantages for a few years. Large-scale agriculture before the war and large-scale industry after the war have tried, with complete failure, to subordinate state policy to the attainment of small, obvious advantages. But the time for small tactics is over. In the coming decades, we will be dealing with problems of world-historical dimensions. And here the economy is always dependent on the level of big politics, not vice versa. *Economic leaders must learn to think in purely political terms*, not 'economic-political' terms. The prerequisite for great economic work in the East is therefore order in one's own politics.

ALSO FROM LEGEND BOOKS

Aelita by Alexei Tolstoy
The Fate of Homo Sapiens by H. G. Wells
The New World Order by H. G. Wells
Early Days of World History by Oswald Spengler

Made in the USA
Monee, IL
04 May 2023

32991204R00095